SYDNEY TRAVEL GUIDE 2025

101 Amazing must-do, Must-See, Must-eat at the Beautiful City of Australia

ALICIA L. JONES

Copyright Page

TABLE OF CONTENT

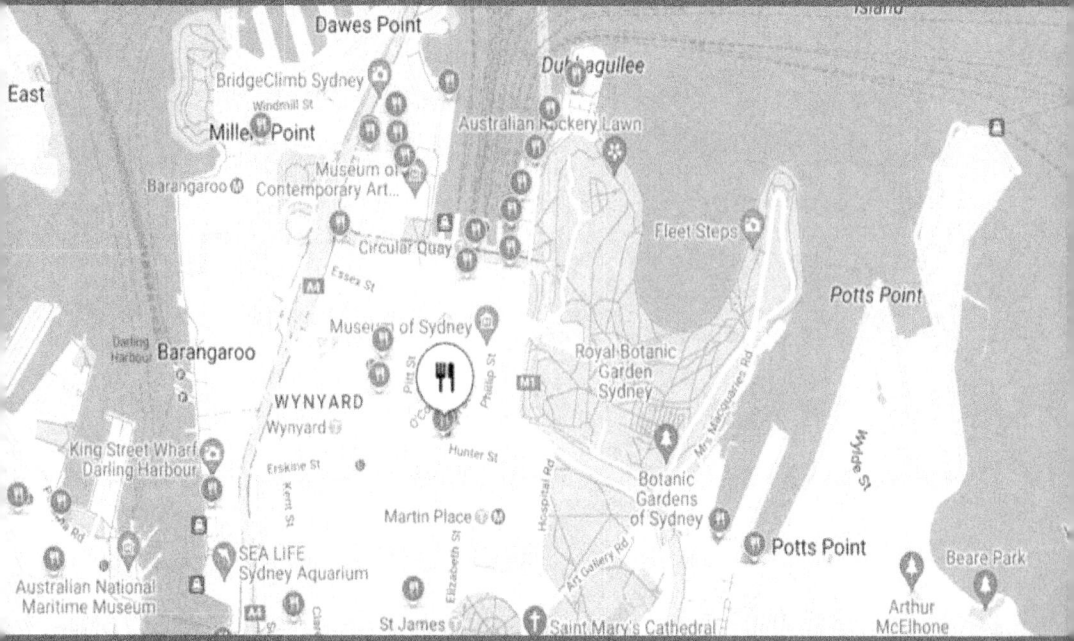

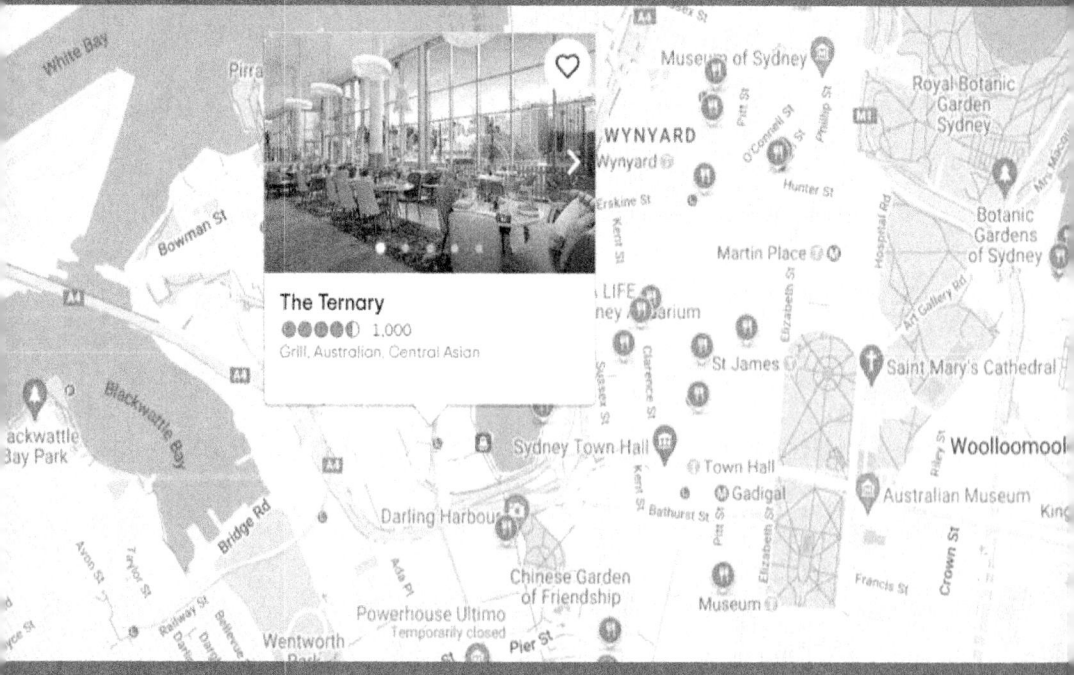

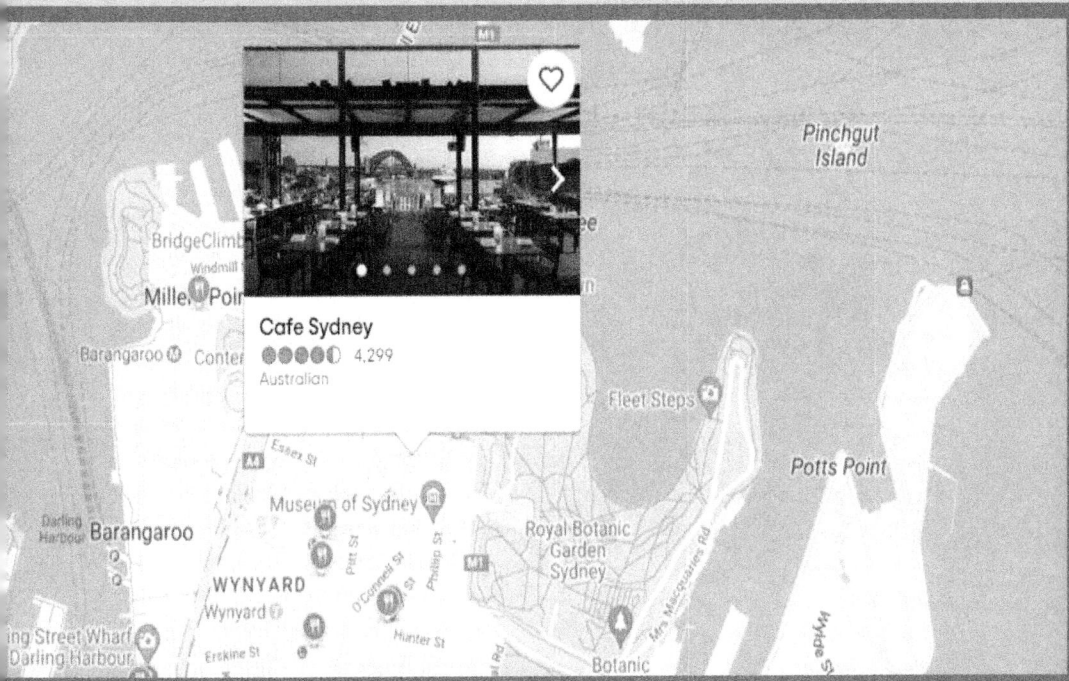

Cafe Sydney
●●●●◐ 4,299
Australian

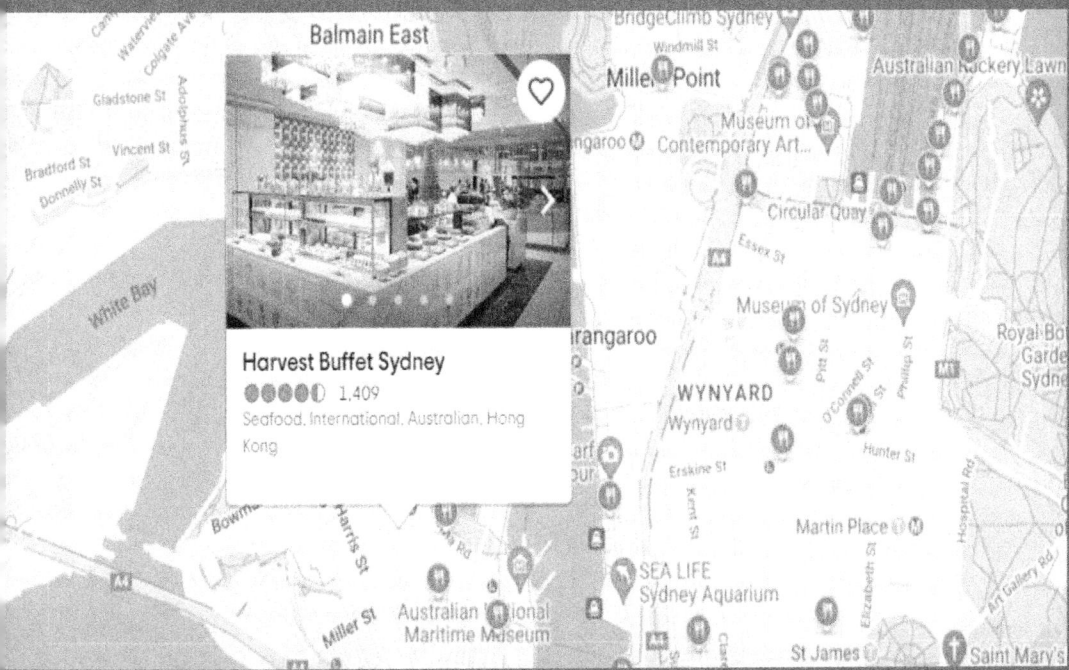

Balmain East
Miller Point

Harvest Buffet Sydney
●●●●◐ 1,409
Seafood, International, Australian, Hong Kong

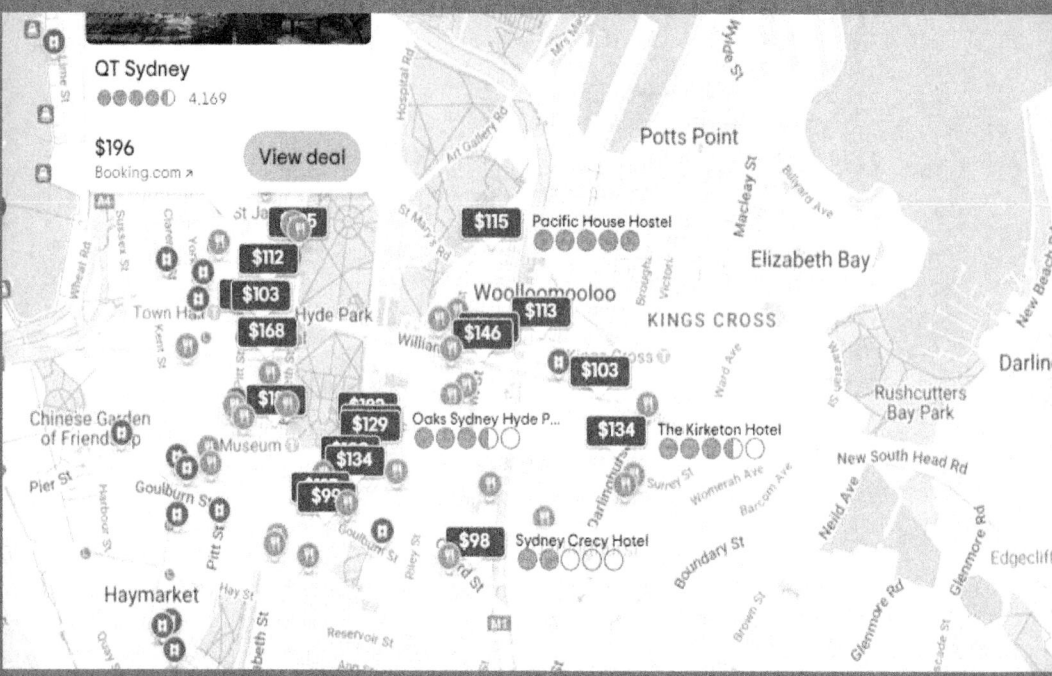

QT Sydney
●●●●◐ 4.169

$196
Booking.com ↗

View deal

Pacific House Hostel — $115
Potts Point
Elizabeth Bay

$112
$103
$168

Hyde Park
Woolloomooloo
$113
$146
KINGS CROSS

$103

Darling

Rushcutters Bay Park

$129
Oaks Sydney Hyde P...
$134
The Kirketon Hotel

$134
New South Head Rd

$99

$98
Sydney Crecy Hotel
Edgecliff

Haymarket

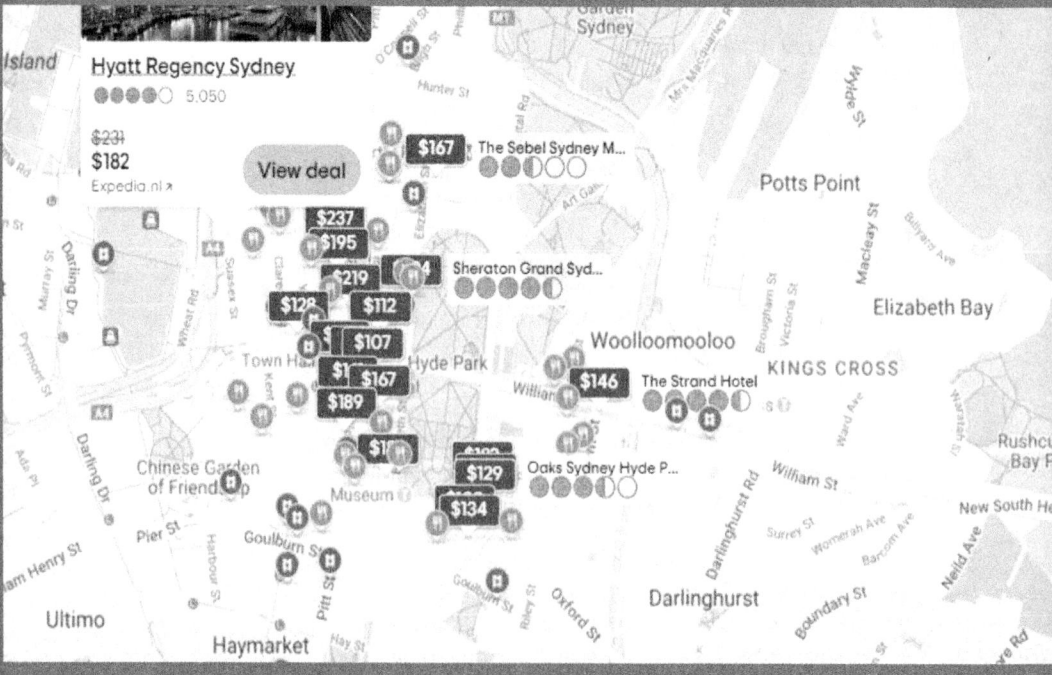

Hyatt Regency Sydney
●●●●○ 5.050

~~$231~~
$182
Expedia.nl ↗

View deal

Garden Sydney

$167
The Sebel Sydney M...
Potts Point

$237
$195
$219
Sheraton Grand Syd...
$128
$112

Elizabeth Bay
KINGS CROSS

$107
$1
$167
Hyde Park
Woolloomooloo
$146
The Strand Hotel

$189

Chinese Garden of Friendship

$129
Oaks Sydney Hyde P...
$134

Museum

Darlinghurst

Ultimo

Rushcu Bay P

New South Hea

Haymarket

Welcome to Sydney the

beating heart of Australia

reetings from Sydney, the beating heart of Australia! You're in for a treat if you've been dreaming about visiting Australia. Sydney offers an unrivaled combination of urban excitement and natural beauty with its famous sites, breathtaking beaches, and lively culture. Sydney is much more than simply a picture-perfect city; as someone who has strolled about its bustling streets, I can assure you that adventure, history, and leisure all coexist here.

An Overview of Sydney Culture

The largest city in Australia, Sydney, exudes a warm, carefree vibe that will instantly make you feel at home. Its diversity is among the first things you'll notice. Sydney is a cultural melting pot where you will come across individuals from all over the world, which is reflected in the city's cuisine, celebrations, and even street art. The city has a strong Indigenous background, and its identity is fundamentally shaped by Aboriginal culture. Sydney has a multitude of opportunities to engage with this intriguing culture, ranging from art galleries featuring Indigenous artwork to tours highlighting Aboriginal sites.

The people who live in Sydney, also referred to as "Sydneysiders," are renowned for being amiable and personable. Locals cherish their coastal lifestyle, so you won't be shocked to find them racing to the beach after work, visiting one of the many outdoor markets in the city, or just sipping coffee at a hip café in one of the various neighborhoods. The city moves at a leisurely pace, yet there's just enough activity to keep you going.

Sydney's Spirituality and Religion

Sydney's population is as diverse as its religions. The majority religion in the city is Christianity, especially Anglicanism and Catholicism, but there are also adherents of Islam, Buddhism, and Hinduism.

There are also a lot of nonreligious people who practice yoga and meditation as forms of spirituality. Whether you're visiting opulent buildings like St. Mary's Cathedral or the tranquil Nan Tien Buddhist Temple just outside the city, there are plenty of religious and spiritual attractions to explore.

You'll feel at home in Sydney regardless of your origins or religious views because the city embraces diversity. Holidays like as Ramadan, Diwali, and Lunar New Year are widely celebrated, contributing to the city's diverse cultural fabric.

A Brief History of Sydney

Sydney's history started long before European settlers showed up. The Indigenous people of the Eora Nation have lived on this area for more than 60,000 years. Their strong ties to the land are evident all across the city, with the harbor and its environs having spiritual and cultural importance.

The British established Sydney as a penal colony in 1788, which is when modern Australia's colonial history began. Changes began with the First Fleet's arrival, and over the ensuing centuries, Sydney developed into the thriving metropolis it is today.

In this metropolis, gothic landmarks like the Sydney Opera House coexist with more contemporary skyscrapers and architectural marvels like The Rocks, a conserved enclave showing colonial architecture.

The Australian Dollar and Exchange Advice

Australia uses the Australian Dollar (AUD) as its currency, and most Sydney locations accept a variety of payment options. Most places take credit cards, even for modest purchases like a bus ticket or a coffee. Still, it's always a good idea to have some cash on hand, particularly for larger cities or street markets where card readers might not be as dependable.

ATMs are widely available, and the exchange rates at the airport are usually fair. However, you can receive a better bargain if you take out cash straight from an ATM that is partnered with your home bank.

Rules and Visitor Safety Advice

Although Sydney is a fairly safe city, it's a good idea to be informed of the laws and conventions that apply there.

When it comes to smoking and drinking, Australia is very rigid. Should you intend to partake in a beverage at any of the numerous pubs or bars inside the city, you must bear identification as the legal drinking age is 18. Be aware of the signage as most public sites, including beaches and outdoor dining areas, have smoking bans.

The importance placed on sun safety is one item that may surprise you. Even on milder days, the Australian sun can be intense, thus residents consider wearing hats and sunscreen essential. Remember to put on a shirt, apply sunscreen, and put on a hat—or, as the locals say, slip, slop, and slap!

Navigating public transit is simple, and the Opal card system in Sydney is compatible with buses, trains, ferries, and light rail. Most convenience stores offer Opal cards for free, which you may load up as you go.

Additional Things to Know Before You Go

It is strictly forbidden to import any food, plants, or animal products into Australia without first verifying the regulations on biosecurity. Heavy fines may be imposed for even the tiniest infringement.

It's usually wise to declare anything you're not sure about at customs.

Last but not least, Sydney is renowned for its outdoor lifestyle, so bring your sense of adventure, good walking shoes, and swimwear. There are many ways to take in Sydney's natural beauty, from strolling along the shore near Bondi and Manly to taking a ferry over the glistening harbor.

This city will win you over whether you choose to climb the Sydney Harbour Bridge, discover the fascinating history of The Rocks, or just relax on Bondi Beach's dunes. Prepare yourself for an exciting trip that will also provide leisure and memories that you will carry with you for a long time. Sydney is a sensation, not just a place, and I can't wait for you to experience it for yourself.

ONE EXPOSURE COULD BE THE ANSWER TO THAT AGE-LONG VOID

KNOWN AND UNKNOWN

FACTS ABOUT SYDNEY

TO MAKE YOU LOOK

LIKE A LOCAL

Sydney Opera House: The Opera House, one of the most famous structures in the world, is a UNESCO World Heritage site and boasts more than a million tiles on its roof.

Sydney Harbour Bridge is the world's biggest steel arch bridge, and residents lovingly refer to it as "The Coathanger" because of its exhilarating rise and expansive city views.

First European Settlement: Sydney, the oldest city in Australia, was the location of the first European settlement when it was founded by the British in 1788.

More than 100 Beautiful Beaches: Sydney has more than 100 beautiful beaches, including well-known ones like Bondi, Manly, and Coogee, which are perfect for sunbathing and surfing.

Aboriginal Heritage: Discover the rich history of the Eora Nation, home to the Indigenous Gadigal people who have resided in the Sydney region for over 60,000 years, during one of the many cultural tours available.

The Royal Botanic Garden, located in the center of the city, has over 7,500 plant types, including rare and endangered ones, and provides a tranquil haven for visitors.

Sydney Tower Eye: Standing at 309 meters, the Sydney Tower is the city's tallest building, providing a 360-degree view of the port, the skyline, and surrounding areas.

Wildlife in the City: Taronga Zoo and neighboring nature reserves are good places to see native fauna, including kangaroos, koalas, and even penguins.

Sydney is transformed into a vibrant, lit wonderland for the annual Vivid Sydney festival of light, music, and ideas. Notable monuments such as the Opera House are illuminated with light projections.

Australia's Oldest Museum: Established in 1827, the Australian Museum provides interesting insights into Indigenous cultures and natural history.

Sydney is known as a surfing paradise, and Bondi Beach is the site of international surfing championships as well as introductory surf classes.

One of the biggest fish markets in the world, Sydney Fish Market offers cookery lessons in addition to sampling fresh seafood.

The World's Largest Natural Harbor is Sydney Harbour, which is ideal for picturesque ferry trips due to its glistening blue seas and verdant surroundings.

The location of Sydney's Luna Park, a well-known historic amusement park with rides and entertainment for all ages, is known for its smiling entrance.

The Rocks: First settled by Europeans, this ancient neighborhood along the waterfront has colonial architecture, cobblestone streets, and a rich history.

Australia Day: Sydney throws a huge celebration on January 26th, featuring cultural acts all around the city and fireworks over the harbor.

Sydney Mardi Gras: Gay and Lesbian Event Sydney's Mardi Gras, one of the biggest LGBTQIA+ pride events globally, attracts people from all over the world with its vibrant parades and festivities.

International Film Hub: Sydney is a well-liked travel destination for movie enthusiasts, having served as the filming location for popular films such as The Matrix and Mission Impossible 2.

Historic Cockatoo Island: Originally a shipyard and jail for escaped convicts, Cockatoo Island is now a UNESCO World Heritage site with events, festivals, and overnight camping available.

The Sydney Funnel-Web Spider is one of the world's most venomous spiders, yet bites are extremely rare and easily treated thanks to anti-venom therapies. This is despite Sydney being notorious for its hazardous biodiversity.

Located immediately south of the city, Royal National Park is the second-oldest national park in the world (after Yellowstone), with hiking, cycling, and canoeing available. It was established in 1879.

Taronga Zoo with a View: This top-notch zoo offers visitors the opportunity to witness exotic animals in addition to breath-taking vistas of Sydney Harbor from its hilltop location.

A Global City: Sydney offers a tremendously diversified cultural experience with over 250 distinct languages spoken there, as well as sizable populations from China, India, and Italy.

History buffs should not miss the ANZAC Memorial, which is situated in Hyde Park and honors Australian and New Zealand soldiers who fought in World War I.

World's Greatest Fireworks Show: Sydney's iconic New Year's Eve fireworks over the harbor draw over a million spectators each year.

Manly Ferry: Traveling from Circular Quay to Manly across Sydney Harbour offers breathtaking vistas of the Opera House and Harbour Bridge, making it one of the world's most picturesque ferry excursions.

Enjoy Sydney's culinary scene while taking in breathtaking views of the harbor at King Street Wharf, a bustling waterfront dining area with a variety of eateries and pubs.

Sydney Cricket Ground: Known as one of the most famous cricket stadiums globally, it is also used for Australian rules football and rugby matches.

Ghost Tours at The Rocks: For a chilling experience, go on a ghost tour around The Rocks to discover haunted locations and discover Sydney's dark history.

Olympic Park in Sydney Constructed for the Summer Olympics of 2000, this expansive venue currently hosts athletic competitions, festivals, and concerts.

It's a fantastic site to learn about Sydney's contemporary sporting history.

HOW TO PLAN YOUR

SYDNEY ADVENTURE

Making travel plans to Sydney is an exciting undertaking. With an abundance of attractions, things to do, and scenic delights, planning ahead is essential for a memorable trip. I can attest from personal experience—having walked its bustling streets, relaxed on its golden beaches, and marveled at its architectural landmarks—that a carefully thought-out itinerary will enable you to take in the best parts of the city without feeling overrun.

Ideal Time to Go

Sydney may be visited year-round, but the time of year you go will have a big influence on how you feel. It's best to go in the spring (September to November) or fall (March to May) when it's sunny but not too hot and there are less tourists. It can get very hot during the summer months (December to February), and beaches like Bondi and Coogee will be crowded. Summertime may be enjoyable, though, if you appreciate the beach and a lively atmosphere—especially when festivities like the Sydney Festival and New Year's Eve are in full gear.

Remember that the winter months of June through August are pleasant in comparison to many other countries, so don't discount it. You can still engage in outdoor sports and see the city without the throng of tourists; just remember to pack a light jacket for the chilly evenings.

How Much Time You Spend There

I would advise allowing at least five days to allow for a comprehensive exploration of Sydney. This allows you to explore some lesser-known jewels in addition to seeing the main attractions, such as the Opera House, Sydney Harbour Bridge, and the beaches. A week will give you enough time to fit in a few day trips, such as visiting the Blue Mountains or the Hunter Valley wine region, which are both within a few hours' drive from the city.

Navigating

Sydney boasts an easy-to-use public transit system that is both efficient and straightforward. Obtain an Opal card, which is compatible with light rail, buses, trains, and ferries.

I would advise making frequent use of the ferries, not only for travel but also as a picturesque means of exploring the harbor. The view of the skyline from the ferry that travels from Circular Quay to Manly is especially breathtaking.

Renting a car could make sense if you're eager to see the world at your own speed, particularly if you intend to travel outside of the city. However, be advised that traffic in Sydney can be difficult, especially during rush hour. For me, a combination of public transportation and walking is my preferred mode of transportation because strolling around Sydney is a great way to find hidden gems like unique stores and cafes.

Where to Stay

Sydney offers a huge range of lodging options to fit every budget. I suggest lodging in the Central Business District (CBD) or the vicinity of Circular Quay if this is your first visit. Numerous popular attractions, such the Opera House and The Rocks, are conveniently located within walking distance of you. The Eastern Suburbs (think Bondi or Coogee) offer a blend of beach life and city amenities for a more relaxed atmosphere.

Check out Surry Hills or Newtown if you're looking for something cool and artsy. These neighborhoods have boutique hotels surrounded by fashionable cafes and street art.

Essentials for Packing

Because of Sydney's outdoor lifestyle, comfortable, casual clothing is recommended. Having a decent pair of walking shoes is essential, particularly if you intend to take one of the city's beautiful seaside walks. Remember to include a hat, sunscreen, and swimsuit because even in the cooler months, the sun may be very strong. Layers are essential when visiting in the winter, as Sydney's mornings can be brisk but the city warms up over the day.

Bring a spirit of adventure, lastly! Sydney's charm lies not only in its well-known sites but also in the little discoveries you make while exploring. Now that you know these pointers, you can start making plans for a trip that will provide you lifelong memories.

Essentials to Pack for Your

Trip to Sydney

It may appear simple to pack for Sydney because it's a global city with easy access to almost everything. Its unique blend of outdoor adventure and urban culture, together with its unpredictable weather, necessitates careful planning. I've been to Sydney a few times, and every time I go I learn a few packing tips that can help you maximize your stay there without carrying extra stuff.

Sneakers that are cozy for walking

Sydney is a walking city, so I guarantee you'll want to take a stroll about it. Your feet will be your greatest friend whether you're strolling through the Royal Botanic Gardens, over the Harbour Bridge, or hiking the well-known Bondi to Coogee beach walk. Bring along a pair of well-worn, comfortable shoes—ideally something breathable if you're going during the warmer months. Hiking shoes or robust sneakers with strong traction are perfect for hikes along the seaside.

Sunscreen Use

Sydney has really strong sun! The UV rays are greater than you might think because the city is located beneath the ozone hole.

Sunburn occurs quickly since the sun can be harsh even on cloudy days. Sunglasses, a wide-brimmed hat, and high-SPF sunscreen (ideally 50+) are necessities. You should definitely protect your skin and eyes, especially if you intend to spend time at the beaches or stroll around outdoor sites like Sydney Harbor or Taronga Zoo.

Shirts with Layers

Since the weather in Sydney can vary quickly, I advise wearing layers. Evenings and mornings in spring and autumn might be mild, while afternoons can be unexpectedly warm. Pack a light jacket or jumper for when the weather cools off in addition to breezy items of apparel for the day, like cotton or linen. Sydney has a mild winter (June to August), but you should still pack warmer clothing, such as scarves and a medium-weight coat.

Swimwear With more than 100 beaches, it's hard to avoid taking a dip in Sydney's pristine seas, even if you're not a die-hard beachgoer.

Packing one or several swimsuits is essential, particularly if you intend to visit well-known beaches like Bondi, Bronte, or Manly. Though many hotels supply them, don't forget to bring flip-flops or water shoes for sand strolling, as well as a beach towel that dries quickly.

Beach bag or daypack

Whether you're going to the beach or seeing the city, a roomy beach bag or a lightweight daypack will come in very handy. For day outings to places like Taronga Zoo or the Blue Mountains, where you'll need to bring necessities like water, snacks, and a camera, I always bring a foldable daypack. Additionally, it's ideal for holding your hat, sunscreen, and other belongings while you discover Sydney's outdoor attractions.

Travel Adapter: Type I outlets with a 230V voltage are used in Australia. Make sure your devices are compatible with this voltage and pack a travel adaptor if you are traveling from outside the nation. There are too many photo-worthy situations in Sydney, so trust me when I say you don't want to be caught without electricity for your phone or camera!

Waterproof Apparel

Bring a compact travel umbrella and a lightweight rain jacket if you're traveling during Sydney's rainy season (March to June) or if you intend to take the ferry across the harbor, which you really should. Sydney's rains are sometimes heavy but usually fleeting. I always have a little umbrella in my daypack; it has come in handy on few occasions when I've been touring The Rocks during an unexpected downpour.

Reusable Bottle of Water

Reusable water bottles are convenient and environmentally friendly because Sydney's tap water is pure and suitable for drinking. Drinking enough of water is essential because you'll be doing a lot of walking and sightseeing, particularly during the heat. When I travel, I normally bring a collapsible water bottle to save room, since the city is full of water fountains.

Crucial Records

Prior to your travel, make sure all of your crucial documentation are in order. This contains your passport, trip insurance, any required visas, and the airline and lodging confirmation information.

Important papers are something I like to have both digital and hard copies of on hand for peace of mind. For added security and convenience, think about keeping these things in a travel wallet or tiny money bag that you carry with you.

Bonus: How to Pack for Sydney's Magnificent Outdoors

Make sure to pack appropriately if your Sydney plan calls for day visits to adjacent destinations like the Hunter Valley or Blue Mountains. You'll need a lightweight jacket, proper shoes, and a small first-aid kit for trekking. For those outside adventures, don't forget sunscreen and bug repellent. Choose smart-casual attire that will look good both at the vineyards and back in the city if wine tasting is on the schedule.

You'll be prepared for everything in Sydney if you pack sensibly, from picturesque treks to sun-drenched beach days to exploring the city's vibrant culture. Recall to pack light, be organized, and enjoy the journey. Sydney is a city that blends nature and urban life, and if you pack smartly, you can explore both without any problems!

ICONIC MUST SEE

LANDMARK AND

LOCATIONS IN SYDNEY

SYDNEY OPERA HOUSE

One of the sights in the city that you simply must see is the Sydney Opera House. Whether strolling around Circular Quay or riding the ferry across the harbor, the Opera House's recognizable sails are always there, welcoming you inside with their proud contrast to the sky. I can tell you that it's not simply an architectural wonder but also a cultural center that captivates you with its history and vitality having examined both its exterior and interior.

Designed by Danish architect Jørn Utzon, the Sydney Opera House opened its doors in 1973 and swiftly rose to prominence as a representation of modern Australia. Its design was avant-garde for its day and now has a futuristic vibe about it. The setting is breathtaking: it's on Bennelong Point, surrounded by the harbor's glittering waters and offering views of the Harbour Bridge.

It is not always necessary to have a performance ticket in order to visit the Opera House. The Royal Botanic Gardens are close by, and you can stroll around the exterior for free while admiring the white, shell-like structure's intricate decorations.

I suggest going inside on a guided tour if you have the time. It gives a fascinating look into the intricate engineering and architecture that went into developing the skyscraper and lasts for nearly an hour. You'll also be able to have a peek inside a few of the performance halls.

Be mindful of basic manners when visiting—no food or beverages allowed inside performance halls, and photography is typically prohibited during performances. Get your tickets in advance if you intend to see a concert because popular ones tend to sell out. Give your visit at least two hours, particularly if you're going on a tour or to a show.

MANLY BEACH

A Quick boat journey from Circular Quay brings you to the hidden gem of Manly Beach, which has an entirely different atmosphere from the busy city core. You'll notice a more relaxed, beach-town vibe as soon as you get off the ferry, with people strolling around barefoot and surfers riding waves. It's one of my favorite places to relax in Sydney, and I've spent a few afternoons here.

Manly Beach is a popular spot for both beginning and seasoned surfers because of its lengthy stretch of golden beach and reliable waves. If you've never surfed before, there are many surf schools that offer lessons, and the teachers are excellent at getting you on the board. Don't worry, though, if surfing isn't your thing. There are plenty of things to do, including swim, stroll down the promenade that leads all the way to Shelly Beach, or just unwind on the beach.

Part of the adventure is getting to Manly. Enjoy some of the greatest views of the Sydney skyline, Opera House, and Harbour Bridge on the 30-minute ferry voyage from Circular Quay. For the complete experience, it is worthwhile to seat on the upper deck.

When you get there, the Corso—a pedestrian boulevard that leads directly to the beach—is lined with a ton of cafes, eateries, and retail establishments.

Manly Beach is a great place to spend a half day, but you could easily spend a whole day exploring the region and enjoying the sun. Just remember to bring sunscreen because the Australian sun may be very strong. Lifeguards are on duty at the beach, and swimming between the red and yellow flags is essential for everyone's safety. Manly Beach brilliantly encapsulates the essence of Sydney's coastal lifestyle, whether you're looking for action or relaxation.

SYDNEY HARBOUR

Nothing compares to actually viewing Sydney Harbour, which is the city's beating heart. The Harbor exudes vitality, from its glistening blue seas to the famous landmarks that encircle it. I've had the opportunity to see it from several perspectives, including a boat, a ferry, and on foot, and every viewpoint deepens your understanding of its vitality and beauty.

There is a lot more to explore in the Harbour, which is most known for housing the Sydney Opera House and the Harbour Bridge. Taking a ride on one of the several ferries that traverse the water is among the greatest ways to see the Harbour. The vistas are fantastic, whether you're traveling to Taronga Zoo, Manly, or just enjoying a leisurely ferry journey. As an adventure-seeker like myself, you really must climb the Sydney Harbour Bridge. One of the most thrilling sensations you may have in Sydney is standing at the top of the BridgeClimb, which offers you a panoramic perspective of the entire Harbour.

You can wander through the Royal Botanic Gardens or pass via The Rocks to explore the harbor's surroundings on a more leisurely basis.

Both provide breathtaking views of the harbor, and The Rocks is rich in history, with historic colonial buildings and cobblestone streets to explore.

The finest aspect? Sydney Harbor is a place where memories are made. It's always appealing, whether it's shining at dusk, sparkling beneath the city lights at night, or bathed in the gentle morning light. It is imperative to pay this place a visit, and I would suggest dedicating several hours to fully experience it—by boat, on foot, or even while having supper at one of the waterfront eateries.

SYDNEY FERRIES

Sydney Ferries are an adventure in itself, not merely a way to get about. I've done a few ferry excursions, and each time I feel as though I'm seeing Sydney from a different angle. The ferries give some of the best views of the Opera House, Harbour Bridge, and the skyline while crisscrossing Sydney Harbour and connecting the city's major neighborhoods and attractions.

The journey to Manly is the most often taken ferry route, and it's also the one I always suggest. The trip takes roughly thirty minutes each way and offers expansive views of the harbor, cliffs, and open sea. If at all possible, take a seat on the upper deck; nothing compares to experiencing the sea breeze as you pass the famous sites of the city. Upon reaching Manly, you are welcomed with one of Sydney's most renowned beaches. It's the ideal excursion for a half-day or full-day.

The ferries connect Manly to Watsons Bay, Parramatta, and Taronga Zoo, among other fantastic locations. Every path has a different landscape to offer.

For instance, you may view the bridge in all its splendor as you drive past the Opera House on your way to Taronga Zoo. You can catch a view of the Pacific Ocean and the Sydney Heads while traveling to Watsons Bay.

The primary center, Circular Quay, makes it simple to board one of the several Ferries that sail. Since the fares are integrated into the Opal card system, you may easily tap on and off the ferries if you currently use public transportation. Just a heads up: if you want a more tranquil ride, try scheduling your trip for mid-morning or early afternoon. The boats can get crowded during peak hours and on weekends.

A Sydney Ferry ride is a need whether you're traveling, touring, or just wanting to take in the beauty of the harbor. It's among the greatest ways to see the city, inexpensive, and soothing.

SYDNEY HARBOUR

BRIDGE

One of those sites that really lives up to the hype is the Sydney Harbour Bridge. I have been in awe of its immense size and the views it provides on three separate occasions—walking across it, driving over it, and even climbing to the summit. Locals refer to this engineering marvel, which connects Sydney's north and south shores, as "The Coathanger" due to its unique design. It was built in 1932. The Bridge, which you may stand atop or admire from a distance, is a well-known representation of Sydney's skyline.

When recommending something to first-time tourists, I usually suggest walking across the Harbour Bridge. On the eastern side is a pedestrian walkway with breathtaking views. Enjoy breath-taking views of the Sydney Opera House, the glittering harbor, and the city skyline as you get a close-up look at the steel framework of the bridge. It's a free stroll that takes 20 to 30 minutes one way, but remember to pack your camera so you can catch beautiful views.

The Bridge Climb is an absolute must if you're game for a little more adventure. Reaching the bridge's pinnacle is a once-in-a-lifetime event.

The guided climb takes around three and a half hours overall, and although it involves some work, the payoff is incomparable. 360-degree views of the entire city are available from the summit, which is located 134 meters above the harbor. It's thrilling, and there's no better feeling of accomplishment than reaching the top.

Check out the Pylon Lookout for an alternative viewpoint. Situated on the bridge's southeast pylon, it provides breathtaking views without requiring a strenuous physical ascent. A tiny museum that chronicles the bridge's construction may be found there as well, providing an intriguing look into the technical achievement that went into building this well-known building.

A trip to Sydney would not be complete without seeing the Sydney Harbour Bridge, whether by car, foot, or by climbing it. It's more than simply a bridge; it's a viewpoint, an adventure, and a portion of the city's past combined.

ROYAL BOTANIC GARDEN

SYDNEY

Sydney's Royal Botanic Garden is like entering a tranquil oasis in the heart of the busy metropolis. Its beauty and tranquility never cease to astound me, even after numerous walks along its paths. Situated in close proximity to the Sydney Opera House, the garden presents an exceptional opportunity to relish the city skyline and the harbor, rendering it an ideal location for unwinding, having a picnic, or simply strolling at your own pace.

Thousands of plant varieties, many of which are unique to Australia, may be found in the enormous, 30-hectare luxuriant garden. Towering palm trees and exquisite flowers can be found, and if you're lucky, you can even catch a glimpse of some of the local fauna, such as water dragons or cockatoos, lounging in the sun. Many of the plant beds in the garden include labels explaining the origins and significance of the plants, making it an excellent site to learn about Australia's unique flora.

The Palace Rose Garden is one of my favorite spots because of the vivid blossoms and heady rose aroma. It's a wonderful place to relax and take in the scenery.

There's always something new to discover in The Calyx, a spectacular glasshouse structure within the park that frequently features different exhibitions focused on flora and sustainability.

Another feature is the stroll around Mrs. Macquarie's Chair. This well-known bench made of sandstone, which dates back to the 1800s, provides a breathtaking view of the harbor, the Opera House, and the Harbour Bridge. It's the kind of place where you want to stop and just observe everything.

The Royal Botanic Garden is simple to fit into any schedule because it is free to access and open all year round. The garden offers the ideal fusion of nature, history, and breathtaking vistas, making it the perfect destination for someone seeking a tranquil getaway in the middle of the city or someone who is an avid gardener.

Queen Victoria Building (QVB)

QUEEN VICTORIA BUILDING (QVB)

One of Sydney's most prized architectural treasures is the Queen Victoria Building (QVB), and each time I come, I am reminded of how skillfully it combines modern luxury with heritage. Constructed in the late 1800s, this imposing Romanesque-style structure was first intended to serve as a marketplace. However, it has subsequently undergone a metamorphosis into a premier retail destination. Its exquisite hallways transport you back in time with to their stained-glass windows, mosaic flooring, and elaborate iron railings that evoke a bygone era.

In the center of Sydney's CBD, the QVB occupies an entire city block, and one of its most noticeable characteristics is its unusual domed roof. High-end boutiques, designer shops, and artisanal stores abound inside the structure, selling everything from jewelry and apparel to gourmet teas and chocolates. But even if you don't want to shop, it's still worthwhile to go for the architecture alone. A visual feast may be found in the elaborate masonry detailing, the opulent staircases, and the exquisite clock installations.

The Great Australian Clock, a gigantic clock suspended from the ceiling that uses elaborate dioramas to depict the tale of Australian history, is one of the most remarkable aspects of the QVB. Every hour, the Royal Clock nearby puts on an animated figure display that never fails to draw large crowds. In addition to being useful, these clocks are works of art that capture the rich past of the structure.

There are a number of cafes in the QVB where you can take a break from shopping, relax with a coffee, and take in the classy ambiance. A popular for its afternoon tea service, the top-floor Tea Room is the ideal place to feel a little opulent in this historic environment.

Sydney visitors should not miss the Queen Victoria Building, whether they are there for the architecture, the shopping, or simply to take in the history. It is a location where history and modernity collide, and it never fails to enthrall.

DARLING HARBOUR

One of Sydney's liveliest waterfront areas is Darling Harbour, and I'm always drawn to its energetic vibe. Situated within a short stroll from the city center, it serves as a center for cultural, culinary, and entertainment activities. There's always something new to discover when I go, be it a thrilling event, a brand-new eatery, or just taking in the breathtaking views of the harbor.

The abundance of things to do in Darling Harbour is one of its unique qualities. The region is ideal for guests of all ages because it has a variety of attractions. Families will enjoy visiting the iconic Australian animals like kangaroos and koalas at WILD LIFE Sydney Zoo or getting up close and personal with Australia's aquatic life at SEA LIFE Sydney Aquarium. The Australian National Maritime Museum has amazing displays on Australia's maritime history, and you can even board historic ships if history is your thing.

Darling Harbour is a terrific spot to unwind in addition to its many attractions. There are several outdoor cafes and restaurants along the promenade where you may relax and watch the boats pass by. The eating options are varied, offering anything from fresh seafood to foreign cuisine, whether you're looking for a casual or more formal supper. I've enjoyed a few great dinners here, particularly in the evenings when the area is illuminated by lights that reflect off the sea.

Don't miss the Darling Harbour Fireworks, which take place every weekend if you're visiting at night. A wonderful way to cap off the day is to watch the vibrant spectacle light up the sky. It's worth seeing what's going on when you visit the port because it's home to festivals and events all year long.

I usually suggest taking a trip to the Chinese Garden of Friendship, which is a serene haven amidst the busy neighborhood. With its koi ponds, classic pavilions, and lush vegetation, the lovely garden provides a tranquil haven from the bustling waterfront.

Darling Harbour offers something for everyone, whether you're in the mood for dining, sightseeing, or just taking a leisurely stroll by the sea. It's the kind of site where you can go for a whole day and never run out of things to do, and it really captures the vibrant, multicultural essence of Sydney.

BONDI BEACH

Unquestionably, one of Sydney's most recognizable locations is Bondi Beach. I could see why Bondi is so popular with both locals and visitors the moment I stepped foot on its beautiful sands. Bondi offers something for everyone, whether you're a surfer hunting for the ideal wave, a sun seeker trying to unwind, or just someone looking to take in the vibrant scene.

The beach is gorgeous in and of itself, with sandstone cliffs on both sides of its crescent-shaped width. The waves are frequently perfect for surfers of all skill levels, and the water is a vivid blue color. If surfing is new to you, there are many surf schools on the beach that give lessons, and the locals are welcome and friendly regardless of ability level. The sight of the surfers floating over the waves is captivating, even if you're simply there to observe.

The beachfront stroll from Bondi to Coogee is one of my favorite things about Bondi. There are many beautiful places to pause and appreciate the beauty along this roughly 6-kilometer clifftop walk, which gives stunning views of the ocean.

The stroll gets extra popularity every year during the "Sculpture by the Sea" exhibition, when amazing art installations dot the beach.

But Bondi is more than simply a beach. There are lots of excellent cafes, restaurants, and shopping in the immediate vicinity. There are several options available, whether you're looking for a light brunch, a casual burger, or something more. Getting a snack at one of the beachside cafes is one of my favorite places to go; nothing compares to enjoying a coffee while looking out at the Pacific.

Bondi is also home to Bondi Icebergs, a well-known ocean pool where swimmers may swim laps as waves tumbling over the edge of the pool. It provides one of Sydney's most distinctive swimming experiences and is accessible to the general public.

Bondi Beach is a must-visit for its laid-back mood, breathtaking scenery, and distinctively Australian beach culture, whether you're planning to stay for a few hours or the entire day. Just remember to wear sunblock!

THE ROCKS

Sydney's historic The Rocks district offers a bustling blend of modern attractions and old-world beauty, capturing the essence of the city's past. Its charmingly restored colonial-era buildings make wandering through its winding, cobblestone lanes feel like traveling back in time. Sydney was once home to many colonial families.

The rich history of The Rocks is one of its best features. Sydney's European colony started here in 1788, and the area's architecture and layout still bear traces of that history. With its interactive exhibits and artifacts, the Rocks Discovery Museum is an excellent place to start learning about the region's indigenous roots and early colonial history.

Both lovers of architecture and history will enjoy exploring The Rocks. Some of Sydney's oldest pubs, like The Hero of Waterloo and The Lord Nelson Brewery Hotel, are located in this region. While you sip something, you can envision the stories of the sailors and prisoners who used to frequent these places. There's also a thriving weekend market in the vicinity where you can peruse handmade crafts, interesting souvenirs, and mouthwatering street cuisine.

The Rocks offers a number of galleries and studios featuring modern Australian art for individuals with an interest in art and culture. Aboriginal art galleries can also be found, showcasing both traditional and modern pieces of art that shed light on Australia's indigenous traditions.

The Rocks is a bustling neighborhood with a flourishing dining scene in addition to being a destination to explore history. There's something to suit every taste, from sophisticated dining establishments to welcoming cafes and lively bars. A heritage-listed building or an outdoor eating area with views of the Sydney Harbour Bridge add even more appeal to the dining experience.

Don't miss The Rocks Markets' vibrant atmosphere if you visit on the weekends. Indulge in upscale delicacies, peruse handcrafted items and jewelry, and take in the lively ambiance while taking in live musical acts.

The Rocks offers a distinctive fusion of legacy and contemporary flare that is likely to attract tourists of all ages, whether they are interested in history, shopping, dining, or just soaking up the ambiance of one of

Sydney's oldest districts. It's a must-visit location that fascinatingly combines Sydney's history and current.

ART GALLERY OF NEW SOUTH WALES

One of Sydney's most well-known cultural landmarks, the Art Gallery of New South Wales is a must-see for anybody interested in art, history, or simply seeing the city from a different perspective. The gallery, which is located in The Domain, provides a tranquil haven from the hustle and bustle of the city thanks to its gorgeous architecture that blends in perfectly with the surrounding parks. I'm always amazed at how skillfully it brings together modern and traditional art under one roof.

There is something to satisfy every creative preference in the gallery's extensive and varied collection. Impressive exhibitions of Australian art can be seen inside, including a sizable collection of works by Aboriginal and Torres Strait Islander artists that demonstrate the rich cultural legacy of the region. It's an intriguing trip through time and culture, featuring both modern and old Indigenous artwork.

Together with Asian and Pacific art, there is also an amazing selection of European masterpieces, providing a genuinely worldwide viewpoint.

The gallery's modern collection is one of its best features. Thought-provoking pieces by Australian and foreign artists abound at the modern art galleries. Since the gallery frequently holds unique exhibitions that draw art enthusiasts from all around the world, there's always something fresh to view. During my travels, I've seen everything from avant-garde installations to Renaissance masterpieces, and the constantly changing displays guarantee that no two visits are ever the same.

With its expansive, light-filled galleries and majestic sandstone façade, the building is an architectural wonder in and of itself. The more recent alterations, which include a sleek, contemporary wing, perfectly balance the historic and contemporary elements. The gallery is large enough to allow you to take your time and thoroughly examine each part without feeling rushed, and the layout is simple to use.

The café at the gallery is a great place to take a break during your visit if you need one. It has a great outlook over Sydney's Royal Botanic Garden and is the ideal place to unwind and enjoy a light meal or coffee. The gallery store, which sells a well-chosen assortment of art books, posters, and distinctive mementos, is definitely worth a visit.

The Art Gallery of New South Wales is unique because it acts as a link between the local and the global, the historical and the contemporary. The gallery offers a varied and fulfilling experience that is likely to make an impression, regardless of your level of interest in art. Best of all, it's free for general admission, making it an easily accessible cultural gem in the middle of Sydney.

OUR TOP PICK IN

SYDNEY HOTELS

THE FULLERTON HOTEL

SYDNEY

No. 1 Martin Place, Sydney,

New South Wales 2000

Australia

009 61 2 8223 1111

The Fullerton Hotel Sydney is a magnificent, opulent location that expertly combines contemporary elegance with Sydney's rich past. Located on Martin Place in the recognizable old General Post Office (GPO) building, the hotel has a rich history that dates back to the 1800s. Every time I walk through its magnificent doors, the building's historical charm is expertly maintained while providing top-notch hospitality, giving me a sense of nostalgia coupled with modern refinement.

The Fullerton Hotel boasts breathtaking architecture. The building's historical significance is evoked by the lofty ceilings, rich details, and spacious marble flooring found within, while the sandstone façade with its tall clock tower captures the majesty of the Victorian era. The hotel even provides guided heritage excursions for those who are interested in history, delving into the building's colorful past and offering perspectives on how it influenced Sydney's civic life.

The Fullerton Hotel offers a variety of opulent rooms and suites that are tastefully decorated with a blend of traditional and modern furnishings.

It's a great location to relax while yet feeling connected to the vitality of the city, as many rooms provide stunning views of Martin location or Sydney's skyline. Spacious rooms with luxurious linen, contemporary conveniences, and well-thought-out decor make for a luxurious and pleasant stay.

The dining selections at Fullerton are among the best parts of the experience. The Place, the hotel's restaurant, has a fine menu with a focus on locally produced, fresh ingredients that blends Australian and foreign flavors. The beautiful backdrop of the ancient GPO courtyard elevates the eating experience, whether you're there for a classy supper, breakfast, or lunch. The Fullerton's afternoon tea, which serves a delectable assortment of pastries and teas in a lovely setting, is also highly recommended.

There's nothing better than The Fullerton for exploring the center of Sydney. It's a great starting point for sightseeing because key landmarks like the Sydney Opera House, The Rocks, and the Royal Botanic Garden are all easily accessible on foot.

All things considered, The Fullerton Hotel Sydney is more than just a place to stay; it's a location that fully immerses you in the richness and legacy of one of Sydney's most famous structures, providing a remarkable experience for every visitor looking for a blend of comfort, elegance, and history.

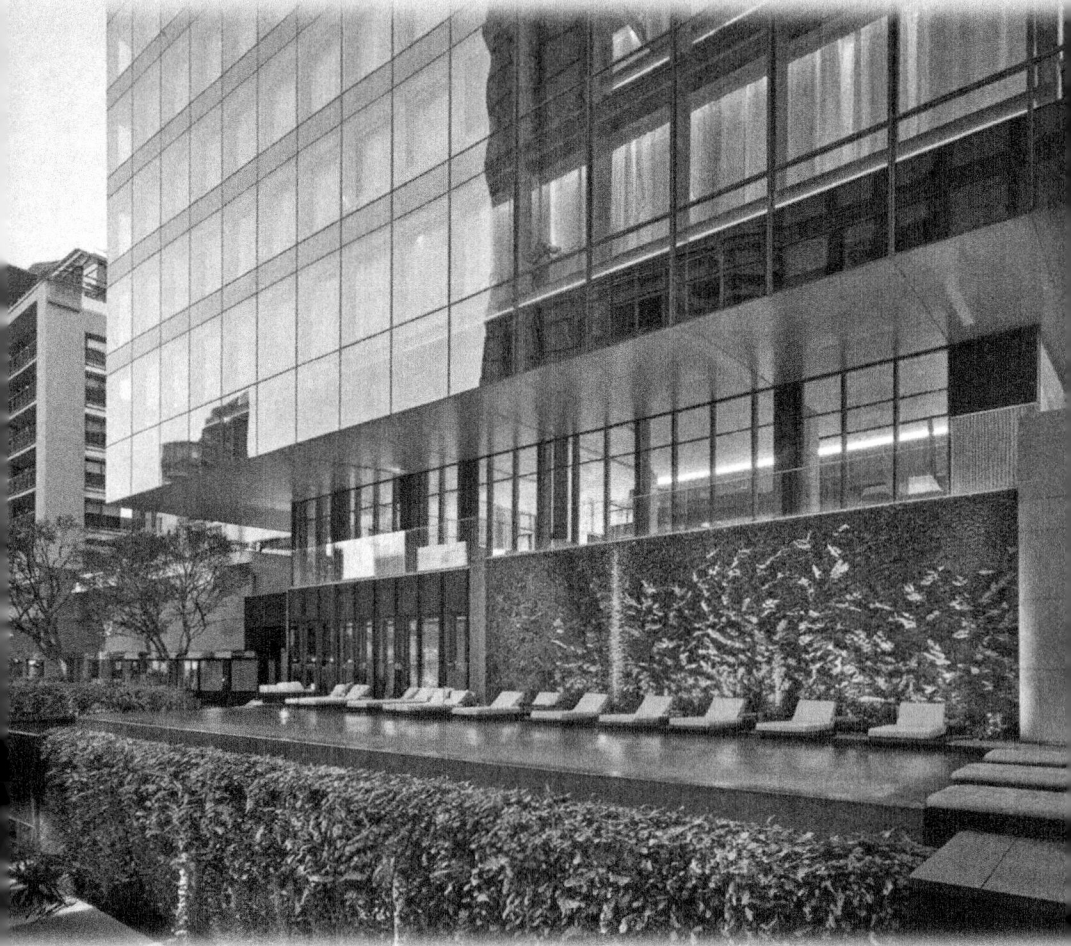

FOUR SEASONS HOTEL

SYDNEY

199 George Street, Sydney, New South Wales 2000 Australia

Four Seasons Hotel Sydney

●●●●◐ 8.842

$240

Booking.com ↗

View deal

Pullman Quay Gran...

$93

$201

$20?

$194

$544

$20? $185 $?06

$206

Sofitel Sydney Went...

$11?

WYNYARD

Wynyard

Hunter St

$220

$166

The Sebel Sydney M...

$186

Potts Point

$152 Nesuto Wool

$116

Woolloomooloo

With its prime position and stunning views, the Four Seasons Hotel Sydney offers an unparalleled experience in the heart of the city. It is the pinnacle of luxury. The hotel is ideally located in Circular Quay, right next to The Rocks and the Sydney Opera House, with stunning views of Sydney Harbour. I've had amazing experiences every time I've stayed here, the sort where you feel taken care of as soon as you walk in.

The Four Seasons' rooms are elegantly furnished while maintaining a high level of comfort. A lot of them have expansive views of the Opera House or Harbour Bridge, and it is very amazing to wake up to see these famous sites. The rooms are large and brimming with opulent touches, such as soft beds, elegant marble baths, and all the contemporary conveniences you could ask for, such cutting-edge entertainment systems, quick Wi-Fi, and a fully stocked minibar. Whether you are visiting for business or pleasure, the area has the atmosphere of a quiet haven in the center of the metropolis.

However, the service is what really makes the Four Seasons stand out. Every effort is made to make each visitor feel like a VIP by the personnel.

Little things like the attentive welcome and knowledgeable suggestions from the concierge team are what really make a stay here memorable. Whether I needed assistance organizing a day of sightseeing or wanted a restaurant recommendation for a special occasion, the staff has always been really accommodating.

The hotel's restaurant is a pleasure in and of itself. Modern Australian cuisine is served up delectably at Mode Kitchen & Bar, with an emphasis on using products that are obtained locally and freshly. And Grain Bar is the spot to go if you love cocktails. After a day of visiting the city, the mixologists create inventive cocktails that are ideal for relaxing with. Take a look at the hotel's wide wine list, which features some of the best vintages produced in Australia.

In addition, the Four Seasons has an excellent outdoor pool and spa, which are ideal for unwinding after a long day. Luxurious and restorative spa treatments are available, and the pool area provides a peaceful haven with breathtaking city views.

All things considered, the Four Seasons Hotel Sydney is an experience rather than merely a place to stay. Its prime location, first-rate service, and opulent amenities make it the ideal starting point for experiencing all that Sydney has to offer while indulging in first-rate comfort. It's a hotel that makes an impression whether you stay for a longer period of time or just a weekend trip.

HYATT REGENCY

SYDNEY

161 Sussex Street, Sydney, New South Wales 2000 Australia

Hyatt Regency Sydney
●●●●○ 5,050

$231 $182

View deal

Expedia.nl ↗

$167 The Sebel Sydney M...
●●●○○

$237
$195

$219 Sheraton Grand Syd...
●●●●●

$128 $112

$107

$167

$189

$146 The Strand Hotel
●●●○

$129 Oaks Sydney Hyde P...
●●●○○

$134

The gorgeous waterfront Hyatt Regency Sydney is situated in the center of the vibrant Darling Harbour neighborhood of the city. It's one of those locations where you may feel comfortable and opulent right away, but it's also quite approachable. The hotel's ideal position allows it to enjoy expansive views of the harbor and is close to many of Sydney's best attractions, such as the Australian National Maritime Museum, the International Convention Centre, and a wide range of stores and eateries.

The contemporary elegance of the Hyatt Regency's rooms is one of my favorite aspects of my visits there. Large windows that either provide breathtaking views of the bay or the bustling city skyline accentuate the modern, streamlined architecture. The rooms are roomy, have luxurious bathrooms, well-stocked minibars, high-speed Wi-Fi, and luxurious linen, along with all the conveniences you might want for a peaceful stay. After a long day of visiting Sydney, you may relax in this kind of place, and the views outside your room can even entice you to stay longer!

Another noteworthy aspect of the hotel is its dining offerings. The hotel's namesake restaurant, Sailmaker, has one of the greatest breakfast buffets in town and serves a delectable assortment of fresh, local seafood, making it the ideal place to refuel before a day of touring. The lobby lounge offers delectable small nibbles and skillfully made cocktails for a more laid-back atmosphere. It's a perfect place to enjoy a casual drink while taking in the sunset over Darling Harbour.

Zephyr, the rooftop bar, is a must-see. It's the perfect place for a drink at sunset or an evening out because it provides expansive views of the port and city skyline. The sophisticated yet laid-back atmosphere and creative drink menu strike the ideal mix for both visitors and residents.

I also value the hotel's meticulous attention to detail in providing excellent service. The personnel is exceedingly cordial and accommodating, constantly on hand to offer advice or extend a heartfelt welcome. The staff makes sure your stay is as easy and pleasurable as possible, whether you are there on business or for pleasure.

All things considered, the Hyatt Regency Sydney is an excellent option for tourists who wish to take in Sydney's dynamic city life while yet enjoying a chic and tranquil getaway because it blends elegance, comfort, and an unrivaled location.

THE GRACE SYDNEY

77 York Street King Streets,

Sydney, New South Wales 2000

Australia

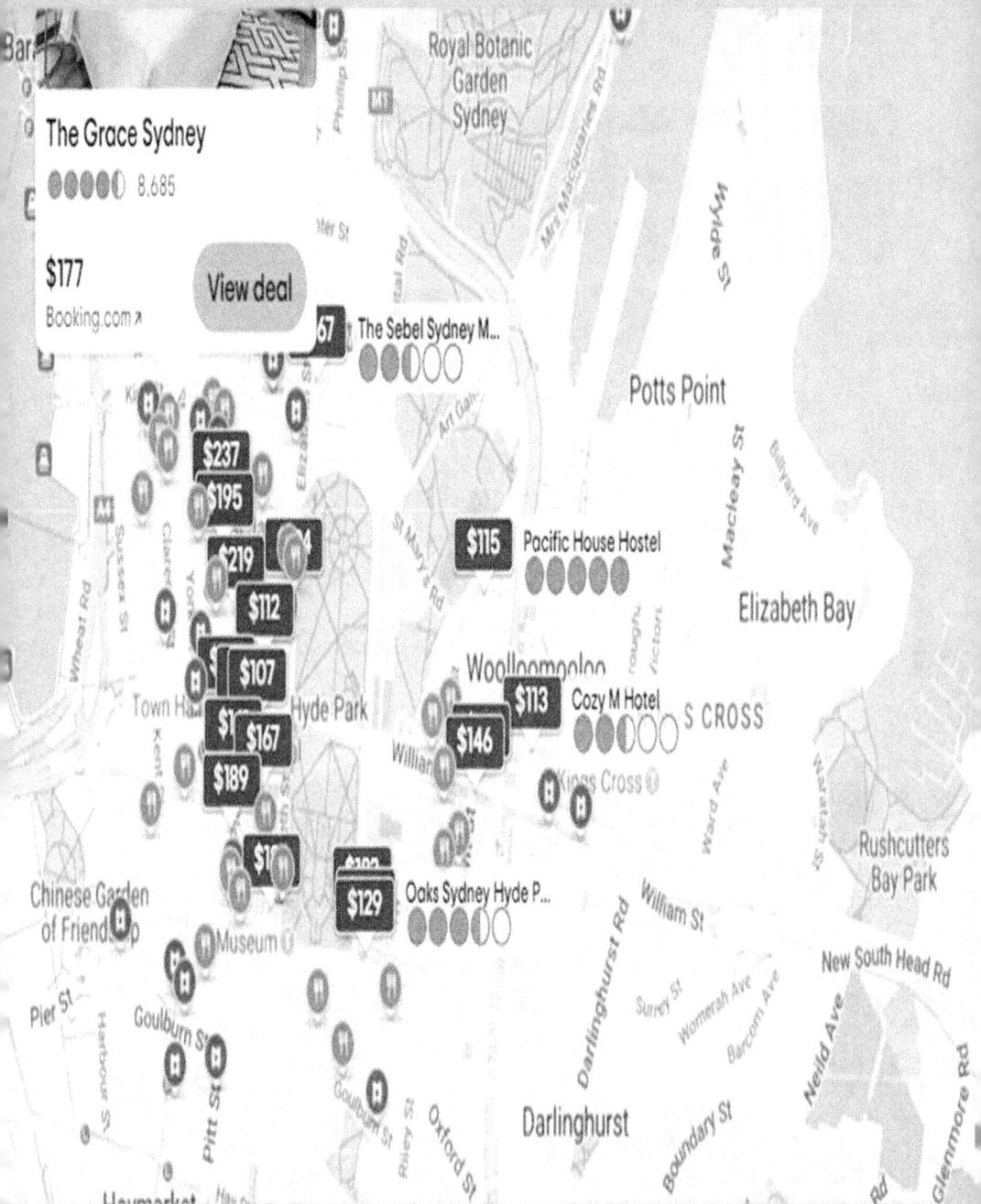

The Grace Sydney

●●●●◐ 8.685

$177

View deal

Booking.com ↗

The Sebel Sydney M...
●●●○○

$237
$195
$219
$112
$107
$167
$189
$129

$115 Pacific House Hostel
●●●●●

$113 Cozy M Hotel
●●●○○

$146

Oaks Sydney Hyde P...
●●●●○

Royal Botanic Garden Sydney

Potts Point

Elizabeth Bay

Woolloomooloo

S CROSS

Kings Cross

Rushcutters Bay Park

Chinese Garden of Friendship

Museum

Darlinghurst

Town Hall

Hyde Park

Haymarket

In the center of the city, The Grace Sydney is a timeless gem that provides a singular fusion of contemporary luxury and historic charm. Situated on York Street, this sophisticated hotel is set in a magnificent Art Deco structure that was constructed in the 1930s. The hotel, which was once constructed as the Grace Brothers department store's headquarters, has managed to preserve its history while offering all the amenities you would anticipate from a first-rate, modern lodging. This resort genuinely embodies the perfect fusion of old world charm and contemporary luxury, and every time I visit, I find myself enthralled with its timeless elegance and modern conveniences.

As soon as you enter The Grace, the opulence of its design catches your eye. With its grand ceilings, elaborate chandeliers, and minute details that take you back in time, the lobby is a tribute to the Art Deco era. Still, the rooms are surprisingly contemporary. Large and elegantly furnished, they provide a calm haven from the busy streets of the city. A well-thought-out mini-bar, complimentary Wi-Fi, a well-equipped fitness center, and luxurious bedding and baths guarantee that your stay will be as fashionable as it is pleasant.

The Grace Sydney's location is among its outstanding features. Major sights including Darling Harbour, The Rocks, and the Sydney Opera House are all within a short stroll from your location. The hotel's prime location makes it simple to see the finest of Sydney on foot, whether you're visiting the city for business or pleasure. Additionally, the Queen Victoria Building (QVB), which has upscale dining and retail right next door, is close by.

The hotel's breakfast buffet is excellent and offers a wide variety of alternatives for any taste, including substantial Australian favorites and lighter, healthier options. Despite the lack of an on-site lunch or dinner restaurant, The Grace's location offers an abundance of options for dining and drinking in the surrounding area. A short stroll will get you to the Rocks district, which offers a wide range of dining options, from upscale restaurants to laid-back cafes.

The Grace's unique quality, though, is its capacity to transport you to a more refined past while retaining all the comforts of contemporary living.

A very unforgettable stay is produced by the building's rich history, the staff's friendly greetings, and the meticulous attention to detail in the architecture. The Grace Sydney provides a singularly lovely experience in the center of one of the liveliest cities on earth, whether you're here for a quick weekend trip or a longer stay.

QT SYDNEY

49 Market Street Corner Of Market And George Streets, Sydney, New South Wales 2000 Australia

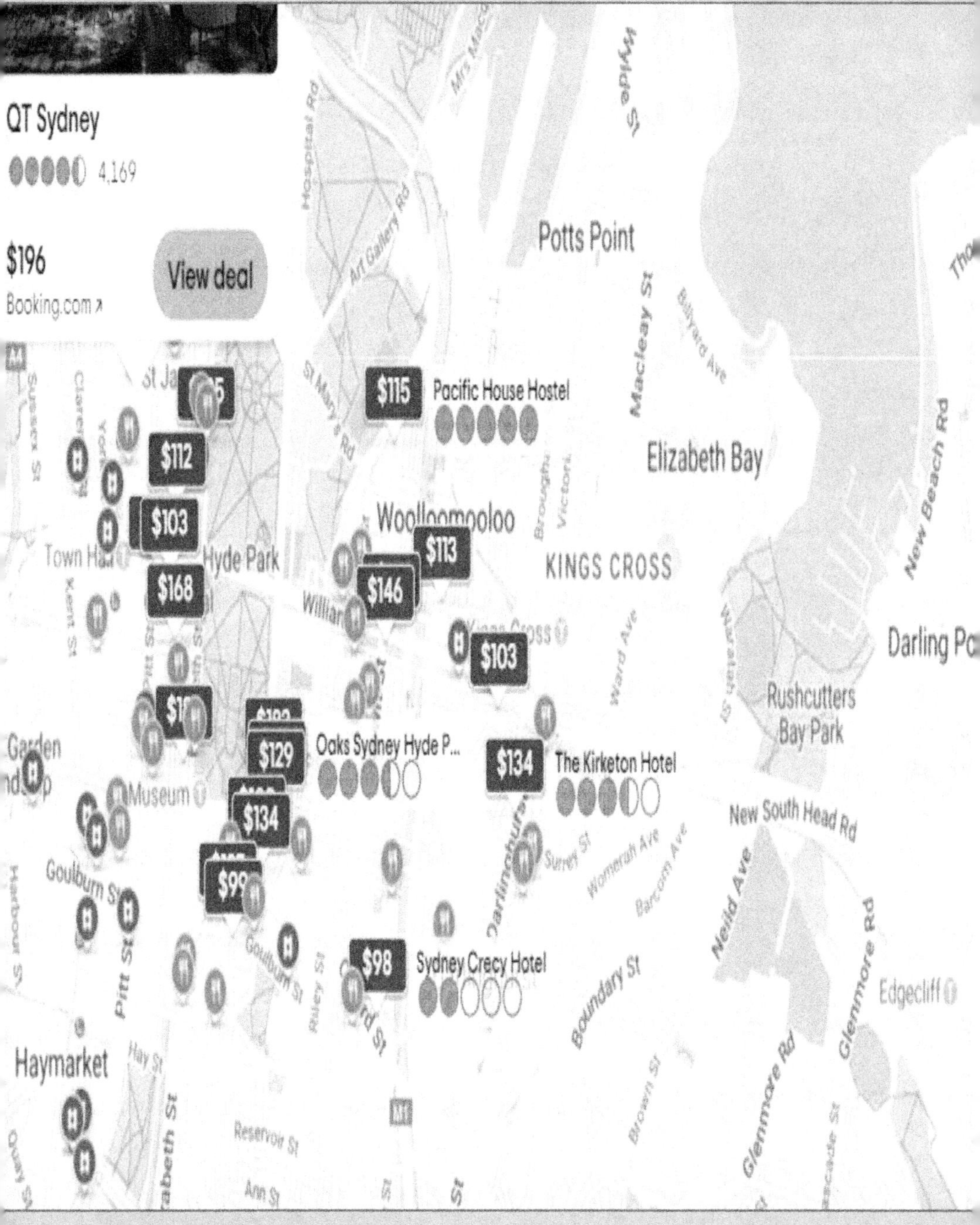
QT Sydney
4,169
$196
View deal
Booking.com
$115
Pacific House Hostel
Potts Point
Elizabeth Bay
$112
$103
Woolloomooloo
$113
Town Hall
Hyde Park
KINGS CROSS
$168
$146
$103
Darling Point
Rushcutters Bay Park
$129
Oaks Sydney Hyde P...
$134
The Kirketon Hotel
Museum
New South Head Rd
$134
$99
$98
Sydney Crecy Hotel
Edgecliff
Haymarket
Art Gallery Rd
Hospital Rd
Wylde St
Macleay St
Baroda St
St Mary's Rd
New Beach Rd
Ward Ave
Surrey St
Womerah Ave
Barcom Ave
Neild Ave
Glenmore Rd
Boundary St
Brown St
Goulburn St
Pitt St
Kent St
Sussex St
Riley St
Reservoir St
Ann St
Hay St

In the center of the city, QT Sydney offers a unique hotel experience by fusing modern eccentricity with historic charm. Nestled within the meticulously restored State Theatre and Gowings Building, this boutique hotel emanates an ostentatious yet opulent atmosphere. I'm always amazed at QT Sydney's ability to seamlessly combine the ancient and the new. The hotel's retro Art Deco façade may give you the impression that you've traveled back in time, but as soon as you enter inside, you're met with striking modern architecture and a lighthearted, theatrical ambiance.

The accommodations at QT Sydney are quite chic. Every room has a distinct layout that incorporates custom elements, contemporary artwork, and vintage furniture to give it personality. Consider mood lighting, polished timber flooring, and luxurious velvet accents. My particular favorite feature is the vast bathrooms, which include enormous soaking tubs and opulent products that make you feel as though you're at a spa. Every aspect of the place is filled with interesting things to explore, from the avant-garde artwork on the walls to the odd details like the vintage rotary phones.

The unique style of QT Sydney extends to its service as well. The personnel is personable, kind, and always wears stylish uniforms that go well with the hotel's decor. The customized touch, however, is what really elevates the experience—whether it's a surprise gift waiting for you in your room or a concierge providing insider knowledge on the city's best-kept secrets.

When it comes to dining, QT Sydney delivers. With a menu that blends contemporary Australian and European bistro fare equally well, Gowings Bar & Grill is a unique establishment. There is something on the menu for everyone, including vegetarian options and fresh seafood, but the steaks are a must-try. For mixed beverages, visit the seductive Glamarama bar, where mixologists create concoctions as distinctive as the hotel.

The location of QT Sydney is something I adore. Because of its location right in the heart of the Central Business District (CBD), you can easily walk to popular destinations including Pitt Street Mall, the Queen Victoria Building (QVB), and Darling Harbour.

The hotel is the ideal starting point for experiencing Sydney since, despite feeling like its own universe, it is never far from the excitement.

QT Sydney is an experience that blends luxury with a sense of playfulness and inventiveness, rather than just a place to stay. Whether you're visiting the area for work, a romantic weekend away, or another reason, QT Sydney provides a novel twist on boutique luxury that ensures an unforgettable stay.

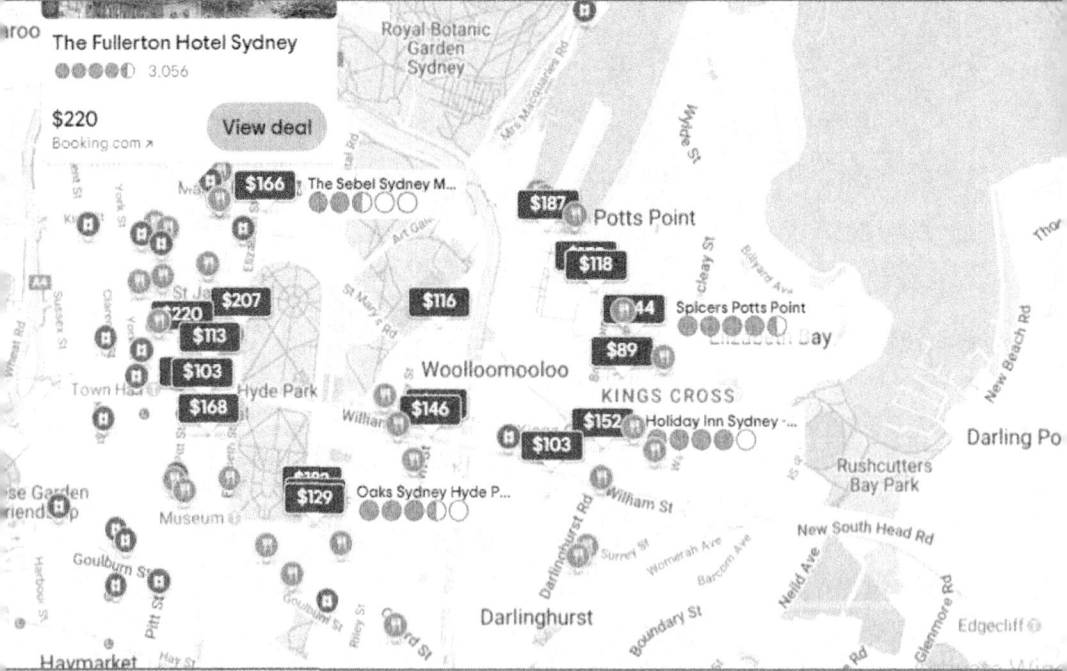

Restaurants in Sydney

HARVEST BUFFET SYDNEY

80 Pyrmont St Star City Casino Entertainment L 1,
Sydney, New South Wales 2009 Australia

+61 1800 700 700

Open now7:00 AM - 11:00 AM12:00 PM - 3:00
PM5:00 PM - 10:00 PM

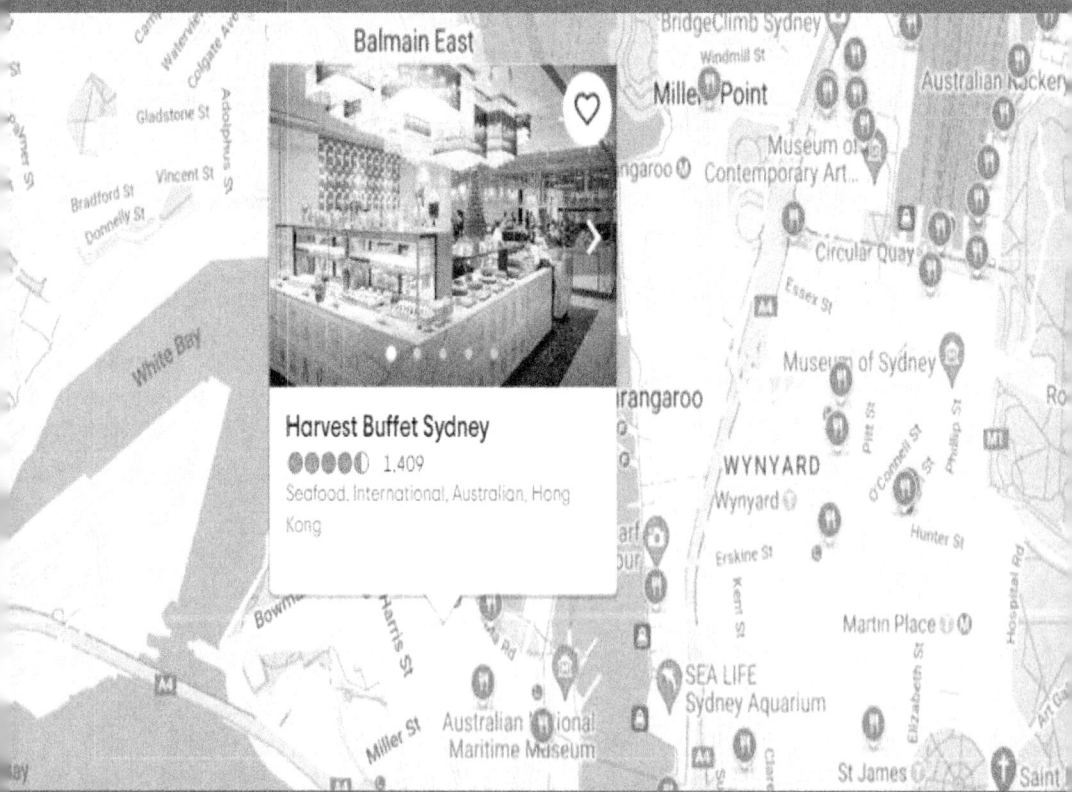

Harvest Buffet Sydney

1,409

Seafood, International, Australian, Hong Kong

Food enthusiasts searching for quality and variety in one location will find paradise at Harvest Buffet Sydney, which is housed in The Star. This buffet is a dream come true if you enjoy sampling a little bit of everything, like me. There is something here to satisfy every appetite, whether you're seeking fresh seafood, Asian delicacies, or hearty roasts. When I first came in, I was astounded by the sheer variety. It's ideal for families and groups of friends searching for an enjoyable eating experience because of the bright, lively atmosphere.

The amazing seafood selection at Harvest Buffet is one of its key draws. Imagine a plate full of freshly shucked oysters, prawns, and mussels that are just waiting for you to dig in. This place is a seafood lover's dream come true. What's the best thing, then? Since it's all constantly restocked, you can be sure that it will be ample and fresh throughout your dinner.

However, it goes beyond seafood. A wide variety of international dishes are available at the buffet. The gastronomic adventure seems never-ending, ranging from fragrant Indian curries and Chinese stir-fries to traditional Italian pastas and wood-fired pizzas.

I recall returning for more to sample every flavor—seconds, thirds, even. To add a bit of excitement to the experience, they also offer a live cooking station where chefs produce delicacies in front of you.

You're in luck if you enjoy a nice roast since there's a special carving station with delectable roasts like lamb, beef, and pig that come with all the fixings. Not to be overlooked are the sweets. Both the eyes and the palate will be treated to a visual feast in the dessert area. You're sure to have a sweet supper that ends with

delicious cakes and pastries and a chocolate fountain (yep, a chocolate fountain!).

Families are welcome at the Harvest Buffet, where you may spend hours chatting over dish after plate of delectable food. Relaxing is made simple by the laid-back, welcoming atmosphere, and the staff always goes above and beyond to make sure you're taken care of.

Harvest Buffet Sydney provides a premium dining experience that blends diversity, quality, and a hint of decadence, whether you're celebrating a special event or just want to gorge yourself.

It's the ideal place to sate your hunger and have a great, informal dinner in the center of Sydney.

CAFE SYDNEY

5th Floor, Customs House 31 Alfred Street, Sydney, New South Wales 2000 Australia

+61 2 9251 8683

Open now12:00 PM - 11:00 PM

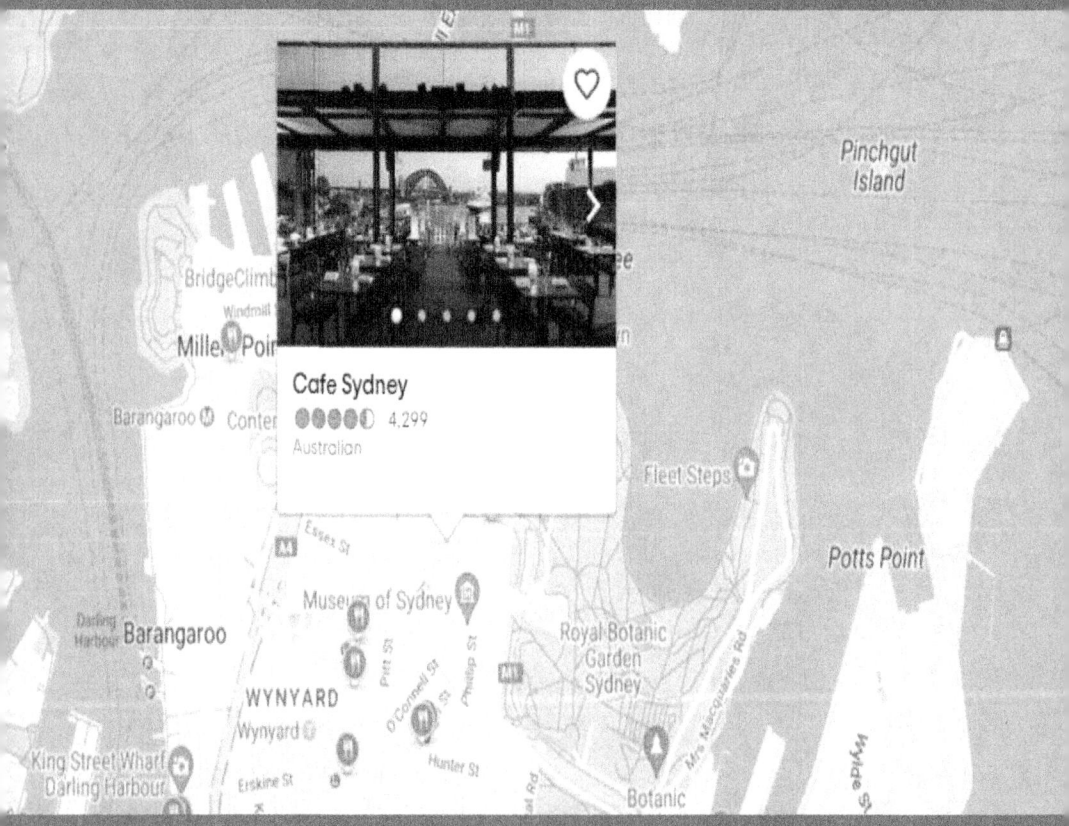

Cafe Sydney
●●●●● 4.299
Australian

One of those rare treasures where the cuisine and view are equally amazing is Café Sydney. Perched atop Customs House's rooftop in Circular Quay, it provides expansive vistas of Sydney Harbor, the Opera House, and the Harbour Bridge. Enjoying a meal here is like living the dream of a Sydneysider—you're not just dining, you're taking in one of the most famous views on earth. Every time I go to Café Sydney, I'm amazed at how the shimmering water and the city skyline combine to offer a stunning setting for an already amazing dinner.

Café Sydney's menu celebrates contemporary Australian cooking, emphasizing the use of fresh, regional products. Here, the fish is excellent.

Everything tastes as though it has just been taken off the boat, including succulent scallops, exquisitely cooked salmon, and freshly shucked oysters. I always start with their famous seafood plate, which features prawns, crab, and oysters that are the best that Sydney waters have to offer. It's a true delight.

It's not just about seafood, though. From expertly prepared steaks to creative vegetarian selections, the menu has something to please every pallet. The barramundi is one of my faves; it has delicate, flaky interior meat and crispy exterior skin, and it's served with a light sauce that brings out the tastes of the fish itself. And their pavlova is a must-try dessert if you have room for it. It's the ideal sweet ending to a lunch that looks out over the harbor since it's light, airy, and topped with fresh fruits.

The atmosphere of Café Sydney is very noteworthy. It is just the right amount of sophisticated and casual. You may take in the scenery and feel the pleasant coastal breeze of Sydney from the outdoor patio. The atmosphere is laid-back yet elegant, perfect for a leisurely lunch, a special occasion, or a romantic supper. The staff always makes sure your eating experience is as good as possible by being attentive without being overbearing.

It should come as no surprise that both locals and visitors frequent Café Sydney. It's a true Sydney institution with its amazing view, great food, and outstanding service.

Café Sydney need to be at the top of your list if you want to take advantage of everything Sydney has to offer in terms of food and landscape. It's the kind of location where you want to stay and enjoy every food as well as every sight of the breathtaking waterfront.

THE TERNARY

100 Murray St Darling Harbour, Sydney, New South Wales 2000 Australia

+61 2 9934 0000

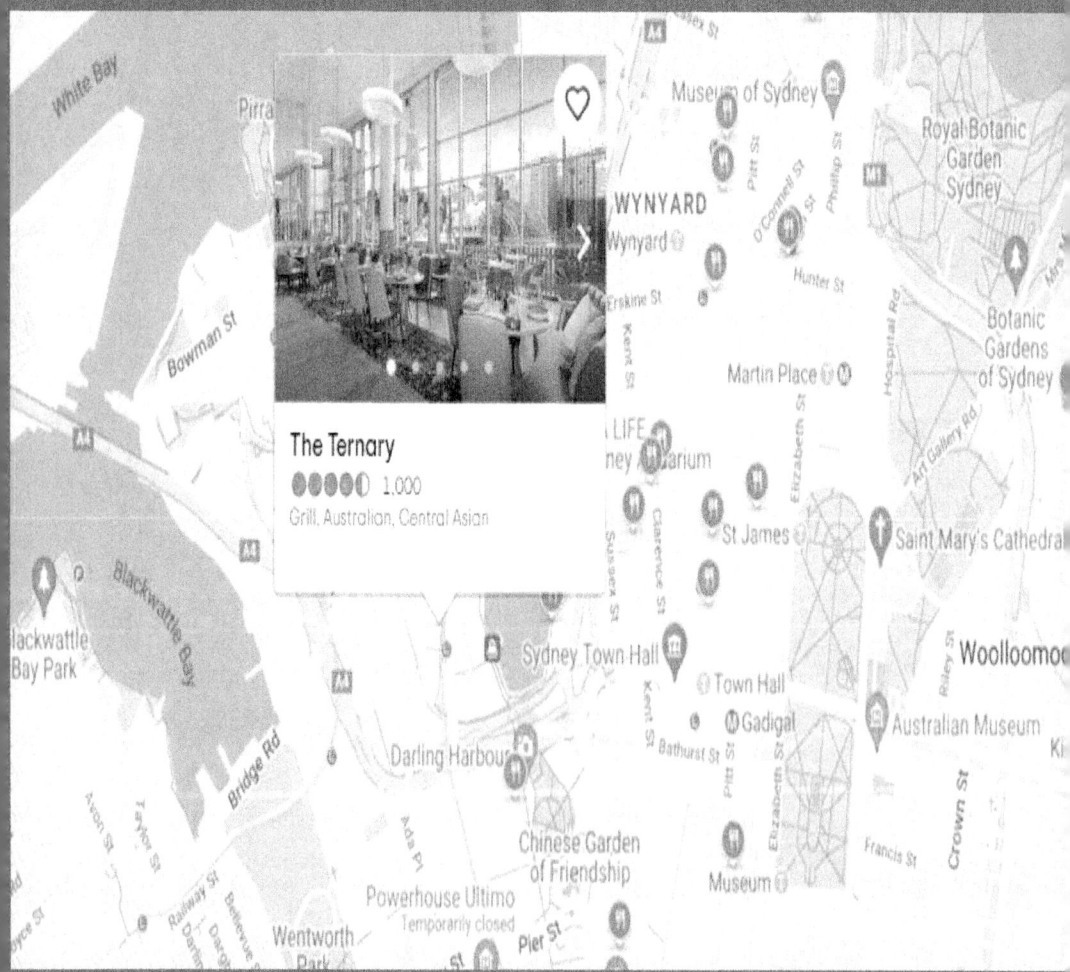

Situated in the center of Darling Harbour, The Ternary provides a dining experience that skillfully combines breathtaking vistas with a vibrant open-kitchen concept. The floor to ceiling windows at The Ternary beckon me in every time because they frame the most beautiful views of Sydney's harbor and skyline. Whether you're having a business lunch or a celebration supper, the lively food and breathtaking views combine to make for an unforgettable experience.

The restaurant's distinctive strategy is based on the combination of three food genres: Asian, grill, and wine bar. There's something even more exciting than watching the chefs at work in the open kitchen; you get to watch your food come to life, from the sizzling of the grill to the delicate plating of Asian-inspired masterpieces. There is something for everyone because to the diversity of cuisines, and I adore how you can sample several flavors in one meal.

I think the Asian cuisine at The Ternary are really good. A particular favorite is the crispy pork belly, which strikes the ideal mix between delicate flesh and crunchy skin.

The seafood laksa, on the other hand, is bursting with rich, aromatic aromas that will take you directly to Southeast Asia. The steaks are perfectly cooked on the grill side, with melt-in-your-mouth interiors and juicy, charred exteriors. A must-try is their trademark wagyu steak, which is delicious, tasty, and served with sides that complement the meal rather than overpower it.

The experience is further enhanced when these foods are paired with a choice from their carefully chosen wine list. There's always a great match at the wine bar, whether you're a wine enthusiast or just searching for something to go with your meal. It provides both local and foreign varieties.

The ambiance of The Ternary is elegant yet laid back. A comfortable yet sophisticated atmosphere is created by the contemporary furnishings and the warm glow of the evening city lights. The personnel is friendly and accommodating, always on hand to offer advice and make sure your meal is enjoyable from beginning to end.

The Ternary provides an unrivaled dining experience, whether you're searching for a gourmet journey or simply a casual dinner with one of Sydney's best vistas. This is the kind of location where you want to stay and enjoy not just the food but also the atmosphere and scenery that contribute to Sydney's unique dining experience.

CHOPHOUSE SYDNEY

25 Bligh St, Sydney, New South Wales 2000

Australia

+61 2 9231 5516

Chophouse Sydney is a contemporary steakhouse that elevates dining experiences with its audacious emphasis on premium cuts of meat and a chic yet welcoming ambiance. Situated in the center of Sydney, Chophouse offers a laid-back yet sophisticated atmosphere for dining, making it a popular choice for both locals and visitors.

Whether you're savoring a flawlessly grilled sirloin, a famous tomahawk steak, or a ribeye, the menu's focus is on honoring the best meats. Each dish is a display of premium, ethically sourced cattle. The steaks are perfectly cooked, with a delicate, juicy interior and a smokey exterior. It's the kind of establishment where the attention to detail and care that goes into every cut are evident. The staff is quite informed and can help you choose the ideal dish from the menu if you're not sure which steak to get.

But at Chophouse, it's not just about the steaks. The sides are equally noteworthy. Consider dishes like their renowned duck-fat roasted potatoes, creamy mashed potatoes, and sautéed greens, which go well with the hearty, meaty main courses.

To ensure that everyone may find something they enjoy, the restaurant also provides a wide selection of vegetarian and seafood selections.

The unique quality of Chophouse is its ability to combine a lively, friendly ambiance with the indulgence of a steakhouse. Whether you're looking for a fantastic meal or celebrating a particular occasion, Chophouse offers an unforgettable dining experience.

7 DAY ITINERARY TO

SYDNEY

Day	Morning	Afternoon	Evening
Day 1	**Arrival in Sydney** - Check-in at your hotel (e.g., Four Seasons or The Grace Sydney) - Stroll around **Circular Quay**	**Sydney Opera House** Tour - Guided tour and photo ops - Walk around **The Rocks** area	**Dinner at Café Sydney** - Enjoy stunning views of the harbour while dining
Day 2	**Sydney Harbour Bridge Climb** - Adventure climb with breathtaking views of the city	Visit **Royal Botanic Garden Sydney** - Relax with a picnic and stroll through the lush greenery	**Darling Harbour** exploration - Evening drinks at one of the waterfront bars
Day 3	Ferry ride to **Manly Beach** - Relax on the beach - Visit local shops and cafes	**Lunch at Manly Wharf** - Take a scenic walk along the **Manly Scenic Walkway**	Return to Circular Quay - **Dinner at The Ternary** in Darling Harbour
Day 4	**Bondi Beach** - Morning swim and walk along the **Bondi to Coogee Coastal Walk**	Lunch at a beachside café - Spend the afternoon sunbathing or surfing at Bondi	Return to city center - **Dinner at Harvest Buffet Sydney** for a relaxed, varied dining experience
Day 5	Explore **The Art Gallery of New South Wales** - Discover Australian and international art	**Queen Victoria Building (QVB)** - Browse high-end shops in this historic building	**Chophouse Sydney** for dinner - Savor premium steaks and enjoy

		- Lunch at QVB café	a relaxed dining atmosphere
Day 6	**Taronga Zoo** visit - Morning ferry to the zoo with incredible views of the harbour and city	**Sydney Ferries** ride back to Circular Quay - Afternoon visit to **The Rocks Discovery Museum**	**The Fullerton Hotel Sydney** - Enjoy an elegant dining experience in a historic building
Day 7	**Sydney Tower Eye** visit - Enjoy panoramic views of the city from the tallest building in Sydney	**Hyde Park & St. Mary's Cathedral** - Stroll through Sydney's oldest park and admire the cathedral's architecture	Farewell dinner at **QT Sydney** restaurant - End your trip with a quirky, modern dining experience

WORD SEARCH PUZZLE

M	A	N	L	Y	C	H	A	T	S	W	O	O	D
S	F	G	H	L	R	B	O	N	D	I	M	P	A
K	I	R	R	I	B	I	L	L	I	E	S	D	R
P	A	D	D	I	N	G	T	O	N	H	T	U	S
A	W	O	O	L	L	O	O	M	O	O	L	O	O
R	C	O	O	G	E	E	A	R	T	U	V	R	N
R	E	D	F	E	R	N	I	A	L	A	I	W	T
A	N	E	W	T	O	W	N	B	N	H	L	Y	H
M	O	S	M	A	N	C	R	O	N	U	L	L	A
A	L	E	I	C	H	H	A	R	D	T	S	T	M
T	I	O	O	W	E	C	C	O	O	G	E	E
T	U	R	O	O	N	S	U	R	R	Y	H	I	L
A	R	R	A	M	A	T	T	A	I	I	L	L	N

Word List:

- Manly
- Bondi
- Parramatta
- Mosman
- Cronulla
- Chatswood
- Surry Hills
- Woolloomooloo
- Paddington
- Coogee
- Newtown
- Balmain
- Redfern
- Leichhardt
- Kirribilli

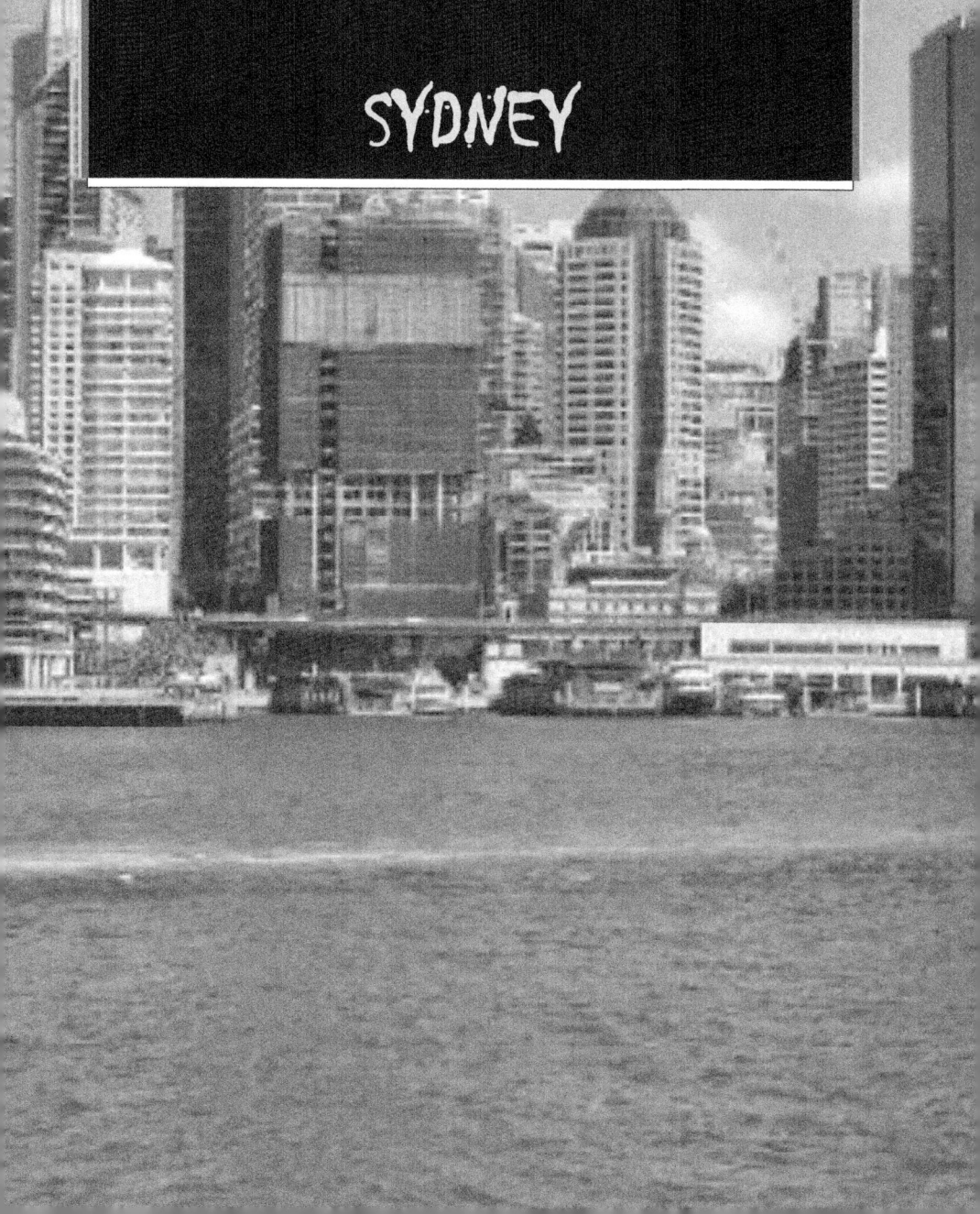

MAPS TO NAVIGATE

SYDNEY

Sydney Opera House

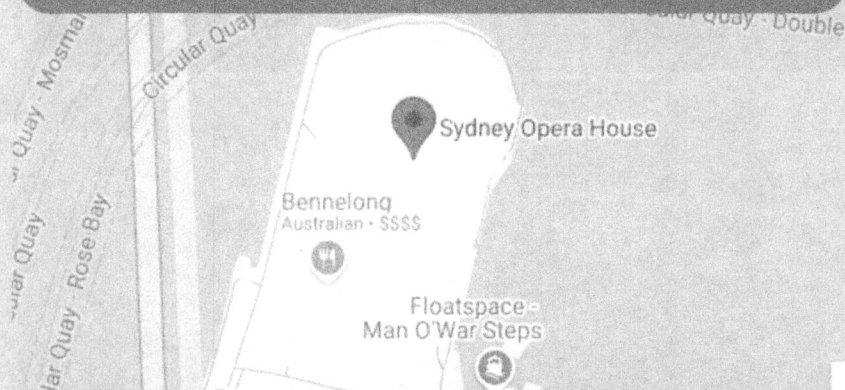

Sydney Opera House

Bennelong
Australian · $$$$

Floatspace -
Man O'War Steps

SCAN THE CODE, LET IT NAVIGATE YOUR DESTINATION

Manly Beach

Steinton St
Steyne
et Pizza Manly
· $$
Beachvolleyball.
com.au - Manly
Whistler St
oke Beach
use, Manly
Francis Ln
Manly Pacific Sydney
MGallery Collection

SCAN THE CODE, LET IT NAVIGATE YOUR DESTINATION

Darling Harbour

SCAN THE CODE, LET IT NAVIGATE YOUR DESTINATION

Queen Victoria Building (QVB)

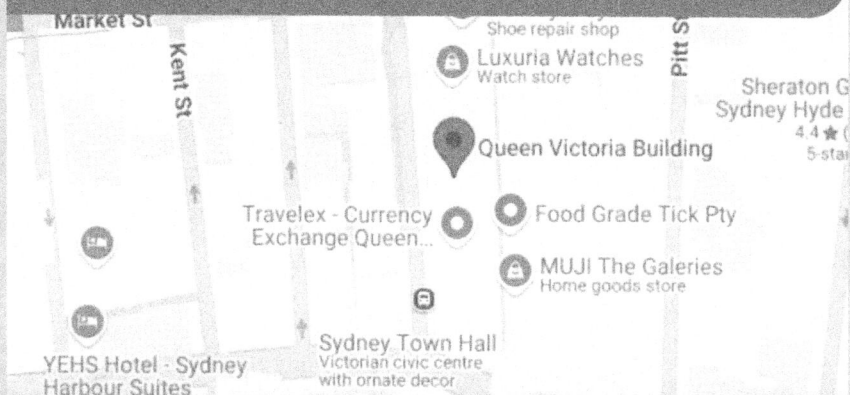

SCAN THE CODE, LET IT NAVIGATE YOUR DESTINATION

Royal Botanic Garden Sydney

SCAN THE CODE, LET IT NAVIGATE YOUR DESTINATION

Sydney Harbour Bridge

Sydney Harbour Bridge
Parramatta
N Sydney - Pyrmont Bay
ngaroo
Cahill Expy
npic Park
M1
Manly - Darling Harbor
Manly - Barangar

SCAN THE CODE, LET IT NAVIGATE YOUR DESTINATION

Sydney Ferries

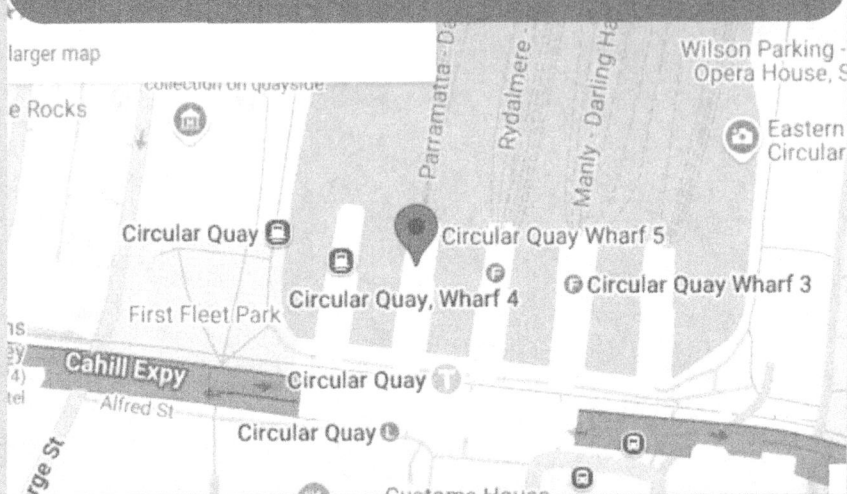

SCAN THE CODE, LET IT NAVIGATE YOUR DESTINATION

Sydney Harbour

larger map

Western Channel Pile
Light/Wedding Cake...

Bradleys Head

Port Jackson Bay

Taylors Bay Track

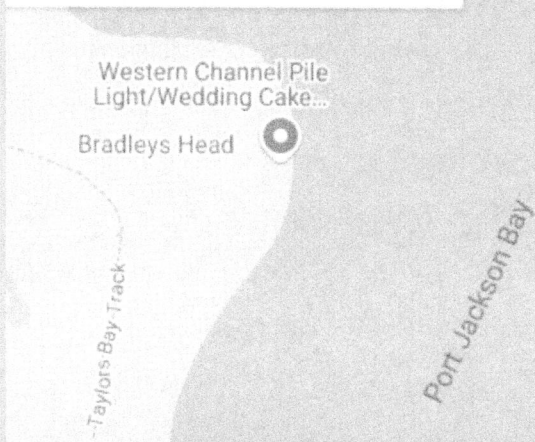

SCAN THE CODE, LET IT NAVIGATE YOUR DESTINATION

Conclusion

As your time with this book draws to an end, I sincerely hope you have gained enthusiasm and inspiration for organizing your trip to Sydney, one of the most stunning and energetic cities on earth. Sydney makes a lasting impression on every tourist with its recognizable monuments, stunning beaches, diverse cultural offerings, and upbeat yet lively ambience. There's always something new to find in this city, whether it's your first or your hundredth visit, and that's part of its magic.

A City With Everything to Offer

Sydney is an experience as much as a place to visit. It's a location where urban elegance and natural beauty coexist together. Where else can you spend the day hiking through the Royal National Park, spending the evening at a fine dining establishment with the Sydney Opera House as your backdrop, and spending the morning relaxing on Bondi Beach?

Sydney is a city of contrasts and limitless possibilities, which is part of its attractiveness.

We've looked at the must-see sights and undiscovered treasures that define Sydney in this guide. We have experienced the ocean breeze at Manly Beach, strolled through the city's history at The Rocks, and gazed in awe at the Sydney Opera House, an architectural marvel. These are only a handful of the attractions that make Sydney a top choice for tourists from all backgrounds.

But Sydney offers much than just its views. What makes the city come to life are the people, the food, the culture, and the lively neighborhoods. Every area offers a unique taste of the city, revealing why Sydney is so lively and varied, from the historic streets of Paddington to the bohemian air of Newtown.

Accepting the Culture of Sydney

Sydney extends a warm welcome to visitors. Its festivals, food scene, and way of life are all shaped by the ethnic influences that come from all over the world.

Restaurants and cafes here provide cuisine from all around Asia, Europe, and beyond, and the city is always hosting events and festivities to showcase its passion for performance, art, and music.

I can't emphasize enough how kind and kind the people are here. Because of their friendly demeanor and easygoing attitude, Sydneysiders are regarded for making city navigation not just simple but pleasurable. People will be delighted to share their insights and favorite sites in the city, whether you're asking for directions, looking for restaurant ideas, or just striking up a chat.

Useful Advice for a Smooth Travel

Please remember the useful advice we've provided throughout this article as you get ready for your vacation. Plan your trip thoroughly, taking into account not only the must-see sights but also the lesser-known locations that will provide you with a more genuine sense of Sydney. With sunny summers, mild winters, and the sporadic downpour, Sydney's seasons can be unexpected, so pack carefully.

Remember to take a look around Sydney's many neighborhoods. Take a ferry to the stunning Northern Beaches, see the stylish shops and cafes in Surry Hills, or spend a day meandering through the historic alleyways of The Rocks. Every destination has a unique personality and has something unique to offer every visitor.

Getting around Sydney is easy thanks to the huge public transportation system, which includes buses, trains, and ferries. Get an Opal card for convenient access to public transportation, and don't be afraid to explore the city on foot—sometimes the most interesting discoveries are found when you venture off the usual route.

The Trip Goes On

Even while this book offers a thorough overview of Sydney's most well-known attractions, keep in mind that your journey never ends. Sydney is a city that is always changing, with new eateries, shows, and undiscovered attractions opening up all the time.

Never be scared to stray from the guidance and conduct your own research. Unexpected locales can yield some of the most memorable experiences.

Enjoy every moment of Sydney's offerings by taking your time. Even though you're halfway around the globe, Sydney has a way of making you feel at home, whether you're admiring the natural beauty of its coastal walks, losing yourself in its rich history, or spending a leisurely evening by the harbor.

Traveling is more than just seeing new locations; it's also about broadening your horizons, immersing yourself in other cultures, and making lifelong experiences. Sydney has everything you could want and more. It's a location where you may experience the energy of a bustling city while still finding peace in the outdoors. This city enthralls with its natural beauty, captivates with its culture, and enchants with its populace.

I hope this book has given you the information, perspective, and enthusiasm you need to make your vacation to Sydney one to remember.

Recall that exploring new things and venturing outside of your comfort zone frequently results in the best experiences. Sydney is a city that encourages you to explore, discover, and tell tales that will linger in your memory long after you leave.

Prepare to fall head over heels in love with Sydney, pack your bags, and grab your camera. There's an incredible journey ahead of you.

Printed in Great Britain
by Amazon

57951968R00079